A History of Women in Politics in Ghana 1957-1992

Eric Sakyi Nketiah

authorHOUSE®

AuthorHouse™ UK Ltd.
500 Avebury Boulevard
Central Milton Keynes, MK9 2BE
www.authorhouse.co.uk
Phone: 08001974150

© 2010 Eric Sakyi Nketiah. All rights reserved.

No part of this book may be reproduced, stored in a retrieval system, or transmitted by any means without the written permission of the author.

First published by AuthorHouse   10/21/2010

ISBN: 978-1-4520-9724-4 (sc)

This book is printed on acid-free paper.

ACKNOWLEDGEMENTS

This work was made possible by the assistance of an endless list of people and institutions all of which cannot be mentioned. The assistance was received also in a variety of ways that cannot all be mentioned here.

There are, however, a few very special ones that would receive mention. These are my sweet and dependable mother, Anna, and her assistants, my sisters, Mr. Jarvis Kwadwo Boahen, Isaac Benjamin Acquah, Mrs Adwoa Kwarteng Fosu and all my numerous friends whose period of studies at the University of Cape Coast concurred with my years as a postgraduate student. I would also like to express my appreciation to my uncle, Mr. John B. Addei for his support and Miss Catherine Arthur and Gloria Ofei who did the typing of this work.

I would also like to acknowledge critical financial assistance received from Professor Irene Odotei of the Tradition and Modernity in Ghana's History and Development-NUFU PRO 34/2002, a partnership programme between the Department of History, University of Ghana and the Norwegian University of Science and Technology. This was at the research stage of the work. All the staff and my former Lecturers at the Department of History, University of Cape Coast, especially my supervisors, Dr. Kofi Affrifah and Samuel Tenkorang and my former Head of Department, Mr. H.K.O. Asamoah are duly acknowledged. Appreciation also goes to Mr. Franklin Egyir, my student and friends at the University of Education, Winneba.

I am also grateful to Miss Joyce Aryee, Mrs. Kate Abbam and Mr. Kwaku Baako Jnr. for their encouragement and assistance. My greatest gratitude, however, goes to my God who has indeed proven that those who put their trust in him shall renew their strength and shall mount up with wings like eagles; shall run without being tired and shall walk without getting fainted.

DEDICATION

This work is dedicated to my mother Anna Ama Antwiwaa Addei (for she merits it). If mothers are indeed a gift and a blessing from God Almighty ... a dependable one for sure.

Contents

ACKNOWLEDGEMENTS	v
DEDICATION	vi
INTRODUCTION	ix

Chapter One
AN OVERVIEW OF THE POLITICAL POSITION OF WOMEN PRIOR TO INDEPENDENCE — 1

Chapter Two
WOMEN IN PARLIAMENT (1957-81) — 24

Chapter Three
WOMEN IN MILITARY REGIMES (1966 – 1992) — 65

CONCLUSION	95
BIBLIOGRAPHY	100

INTRODUCTION

The history of post-colonial Ghana, like those of many other African countries provides several examples of women who have overcome difficult socio-cultural barriers to make an impact in politics. One of these difficulties is the idea that women must be seen and not heard. One would agree with Amadou-Mahter M'bou that, in spite of this chauvinist stance some women have been seen as well as heard. Their trump card has been their sensitivity, tenacity and capacity for sacrifice. Women's role in the Ghanaian society and indeed most, if not all, of Africa was traditionally restricted to agricultural and domestic work; in the tending of animals, the performance of household chores such as cooking, fetching water, collecting wood, grinding, spinning of cotton, and cloth making among other forms of drudgery. There are, however, instances of feminine awakening even in traditional society. Nana Yaa Asantewaa, the famous queen-mother of Edweso with her activities in the first decade of the twentieth century appears to be the most shining example.

After Yaa Asantewaa, Ghanaian women seemed to have virtually gone into oblivion until after the end of the Second World War in 1945 when nationalist movements that sprang up across Africa saw Ghanaian women, especially the traders, joining in the mass movements. Even then, their traditional duties coupled with low education, poverty and inferiority complex made them content with positions far from the forefront of the struggle. They seemed to have been imprisoned somewhere in the world the men had fashioned for themselves.

The issues demanding attention on the eve of independence such as structural development in general and social justice in particular were the same issues that needed to be tackled in independent Ghana. One realistic way of looking at those issues was to take a second look at the role of women in post-colonial society. The efforts made by Dr. Kwame Nkrumah to see many women in politics after 1957 were sustained by the military regime of Flt. Lt. J. J. Rawlings in the post-1981 period.

In between these two periods, very little was seen about Ghanaian women politicians.

The subject of women in politics in Ghana in the 1957 – 1992 period has received virtually no attention from scholars of Ghanaian political history. It is common to examine the political history of this country without adequate regard for the role of women.

A DISCUSSION ON THE CONCEPT OF POLITICS

Edwin Coulter describes politics as, "the public actions of free men and women intent on being heard and involved in public questions."[1] In Coulter's view, "Political governments open themselves to all appropriate opinions and seek conciliatory compromises which emerge as temporary laws or decisions. Politics is an activity- a means to an end. It can take place in simple or complex structures. It is a human, normal process. It is civilized humanity in the fullness of their public being"[2]

To Leslie Paul Thiele, "Politics is often defined as the art and science of government. Government refers to the institutions and processes through which binding decisions are made for a society. Politics, then, pertains to the means employed to organise and regulate collective human existence."[13] All human beings, in his opinion, are under the influence of politics one way or the other. He writes, "Politics is found everywhere that humans are found. No areas of human life are completely beyond its reach or wholly untouched by its effects. To say that there are few if any areas of human life unaffected by politics, however, is not to say that everything is or should be political in the same way or to the same degree"[4]

Thomas Magstadt's elaborate simplification of politics is also worth citing, "... politics encompasses the way human beings in the aggregate govern themselves. Governing implies the existence of a community-that is, an association of individuals who share a common identity. Because the basis for this identity often is geographical....people inhabiting the same region generally are thought to constitute a natural community. Characteristically, the members of a community share common ethical values, religious or social beliefs and ethnic origins. Occasionally, a community can be created by instilling a sense of common purpose or a single political allegiance within the members of an otherwise diverse group. ..."[5]

In Political Science: An Introduction, Gilbert Keith Bluwey describes how existing literature and even teachers in a good number of universities, either completely ignore or give, "only peripheral treatment to most of the basic concepts, institutions and processes of government and politics"[6] Again, Bluwey observes that existing literature failed to reflect "elements in the African political setting".[7] His work, therefore, would correct the anomalies created by a blurred understanding of politics in the African setting. Bluwey was, however, quick to add "I am of course aware that no individual effort can fully exhaust the vast area of government and politics"[8]

The concept of politics defies simplification. This is what has made it possible to have as many definitions as there are political scientists. What appears, more or less, to be a point of convergence is the adoption of and sometimes adaptation to Aristotle's teaching that man is a political animal. Bluwey could not agree with Aristotle better; "Modern man is undoubtedly a political animal" Bluwey writes, "and political activity is a universal pre-occupation in every organised human collectivity. This is so because the average person in the world today, no matter where he lives, what kind of work he does for a living, whether he is single or married, literate or illiterate, or whether he lives in a city or a remote village, finds himself engaged in some sort of discussion on politics every day in his life. If he is thinking about the state, the discussion may range from the conditions of local roads, the school system, the supply of water and electricity to his community, the attitude of a public official towards him, to news of war and peace in places both near and far from his home. On the other hand, he may engage in discussions on the social behaviour of the local minister of his church, or of the mullah of his mosque, or on arrangements for a proposed festival in his home town or village".[9]

Part of Aristotle's teaching is that man lives in organised communities where relationships between one another are regulated. Power is used in the regulation of these relationships by the authorities, rulership or simply the leadership. This is the angle from which Max Weber sees politics and, therefore, defines political science as "the discipline that concerns itself with the relationships of power, rule or authority".[10]

Politics is not political science and political science is not politics. Politics is an art and political science is the study of that art in a scientific way.

Politics, however, is not always scientific. This means that the two are different concepts. It is, however, scholars understanding of politics that informs their definition of its study - political science.

In all the definitions given above, one can see politics as concerning itself with "the overall organisation of society, the modes of creating and distributing benefits and obligations and in general, the best ways of ensuring fairness and order in society."[11]

The plurality of definitions of the concept of politics has made it even the more important to operationalise the concept as it relates to this work. As far as this work is concerned, politics shall be viewed as the activity that has an immediate effect on the state or government. To this end, remote activities like the authority exerted by a clergywoman over her church, though essentially political, would not be treated. Also, the activity of Ghanaian traditional councils and authorities would not receive mention.

SCOPE OF WORK

A history of women in politics in Ghana is, without doubt, a broad subject. One can focus attention on women in politics in the rural areas, women in politics in the urban areas, women in democratic opposition parties, women in cabinet/ministerial positions, women in the organizational structures of poltical parties, women in local government and women in ambassadorial positions, among several other dimensions.

As far as this work is concerned attention would be on three broad sub-themes: women in the governments of military regimes, women in parliament and women in the independence movement in Ghana.

Ghanaian women have played an important role in politics since independence but have not been recognized. The principal aim of this research is to establish the facts behind this thesis.

Again, it is a must to determine the role of women in politics in post-colonial Ghana. There are two main reasons for this:

(i)   Women form more than 50% of Ghana's population. It is inconceivable that such a chunk of the population have not played any part in national politics.

(ii)   The country's history provides examples of eminent women personalities. It is proper that the political role of such women is determined and documented.

To date, no serious effort has been made to do this as the literature review below shows.

LITERATURE REVIEW

It has to be mentioned that most of the literature available on the subject of women in politics be it in Ghana or elsewhere in the world treat the issue from the perspective of sociology or anthropology. Explanation is given to the paucity of numbers in respect of political participation in purely sociological or anthropological terms. Very little recording, by way of actual happenings, has been made. That is to say the historical eye appears to have been effectively shut on this subject. Even in instances where the angle appears to have a historical slant, the purpose is to explain a point in sociology. The importance of the sociological explanations would, however, not be degraded by the researcher because of the emerging trend in historical reconstruction which advises a multidisciplinary approach to the explanation of historical phenomena. It is in the light of this that sociological and sometimes anthropological literature was consulted for explanation.

Dr. K. A. Busia in The Position of the Chief In The Modern Political System of Ashanti touches on the role of women in the traditional state,

"The queen-mother is described as the 'mother' of the chief'. She is more often his sister, but constitutionally she is regarded as the chief's mother, hence her title, hemmaa (female monarch), is usually translated queen mother. She is expected to advise the chief about his conduct. She may scold and reprove him in a way none of his councillors can.

Two queen-mothers of Juaben, Ataa Birago and Afua Kobi, were destooled for not advising their sons (that is, the chiefs) well. When a chief's stool becomes vacant, it is from the queen mother that the elders ask for a man to fill the vacant stool. As the mother of the members of the royal lineage, she is regarded as the authority on the kinship relations of the lineage". The difference Dr. Busia's work has with the subject of this research is that it discusses a pre-independent Ghana situation. Secondly, his is not a work that gives a historical account but merely explains a point in anthropology. The references to Ataa Birago and Afua Kobi are just to explain an anthropological reason by making a historical reference.

Maria Nzomo in a contributory article to Democratic Theory and Practice edited by Walter O. Oyugi et al., has this to say about low women participation in politics in Africa, "Many years of societal indoctrination and psychological conditioning have led many African women to accept the inferior and subordinate status accorded them, thus inhibiting them from challenging the male-dominated status quo. Indeed, some of the African women are aware that they have the same rights and responsibilities as men in society, but they do not have the courage and

self-confidence to exercise these rights. It is this acquiescence, built sometimes on ignorance and sometimes on lack of assertiveness that to a significant extent helps to perpetuate the paternalistic attitudes African men continue to have towards their fellow women citizens." This quotation is not historical in content but it does assign reasons that are deep-rooted in history. As could be seen, the observation on women is general and does not explain the specific case of Ghana within the period this research investigates.

Edzodzinam Tsikata, in a contributory article to The State, Development And Politics In Ghana edited by Emmanuel Hanson and Kwame Ninsin, is not happy with the dominance of political power by males, "from the realm of traditional rule to that of central government... the few women who get into government, although involved in the direct exercise of political power, do not make much impact on the male-dominated character of government". Like the other works previously cited, there is no mention of the names that are so necessary alongside dates or periods to give her work a historical flavour.

Sandra Pepera in an article in Political Parties and Democray in Ghana's Fourth Republic edited by Kwame Ninsin and F. K. Drah states that the political system has failed women notwithstanding their active participation in both the colonial struggle and post-colonial national politics. She writes, "The importance of women's participation has always been recognized, but this has brought little actual progress or improvement in the condition of women in Ghana. The visible representation of women in Ghana is both quantitatively and qualitatively low, and has done nothing to remove the invisibility surrounding women". This was an appraisal of pre-Fourth Republic Ghana. She goes on to provide some statistics in the Provisional National Defence Council era to support what she describes as a depressing situation. "... In the consultative Assembly which drafted the 4th Republican Constitution, there were only 25 women out of some 260 members, and whilst the nine-person ruling Provisional National Defence Council itself has always since 1983 had one woman member, there are presently no women secretaries of state, whilst a few have been and are deputies. There are only two women ambassadors in Ghana's diplomatic corps." Equally important are some statistics she reveals about parliamentary representation in pre-Fourth Republic Ghana. Because this work was not an extensive research on women but one of several articles in an edited work, Sandra Pepera could not, for example, tell the positions some of these women held, the duration of their respective tenures, their relationship with their male counterparts and even how they evaluate the political situation of their times. These are areas this research has tried to study.

Takyiwaa Manuh contributes to the volume of work on Ghanaian women. In an article contributed to Ghana under PNDC Rule edited by E. Gyimah-Boadi, she writes on women in the Ghanaian political economy, market traders and the Revolution launched and headed by Flt. Lt. Rawlings and laws that were made for women among others. One important sub-theme treated in the article is the 31st December Women's Movement, perhaps the most influential Ghanaian feminine mass movement of all time. Takyiwaa Manuh discusses the relationships between the Movement and the PNDC, the Movement and other women's groups, the Movement and the National Council on Women and Development. She then attempts a general survey of the socio-political landscape by assessing the gains of the movement. Though Takyiwaa Manuh takes a look at the 1981-92 period, no personalities in centre stage politics have their names being mentioned. Perhaps the look was too cursory to spot some of the women like Ama Ata Aidoo, Joyce Aryee, Vida Yeboah who were daily newsmakers within the period her study seeks to investigate. Nor was mention made of the role of any of such women in many of the policies and programmes of the longest serving military regime in the history of the country.

Kojo Vieta in The Flagbearers of Ghana writes about such women as Hannah Cudjoe, Mabel Dove-Danquah, Susanna Al-Hassan and Sophia Oboshie Doku and the contributions they made to the struggle for Ghana's independence and in the formative years of the new nation. Vieta also writes about their contributions to the governments that came after the overthrow of the government of Dr. Nkrumah. Vieta's work is sketchy. It does not deal so much with the women as they appeared in those milieux. That is to say his work says very little about the general environment the women operated and what might have conditioned their rise to prominence. Vieta cannot be taken on for he was merely attempting a summary of biographies. Some of his shortcomings notwithstanding, his work would be one of the springboards on which to leap towards an extensive interpretation and analysis of the period.

In By Nkrumah's Side, Tawia Adamafio recounts the history behind the National Council of Ghana Women which was formed to, among other things, help women to, "go shoulder-to-shoulder with our men to advance the socialist cause of progress and prosperity for Ghana". Names such as Sophia Doku, Hannah Cudjoe and Evelyn Amarteifio are mentioned in the work. There is, however, little mention of the impact of the NCGW on the political participation of women. Adamafio cannot be criticized for paying little attention to this. As it turned out, his work is about his relationship with Nkrumah within which the story of the NCGW is a small subset.

Jean O'Barr's article, "African Women in Politics" in African Women South of the Sahara edited by Margaret Jean Hay and Sharon Stichter treats the subject of women in politics. She discusses the exercise of political power by women, their role in pre-colonial politics, their involvement in the colonial period, their role in the various nationalist movements and women as they appear on the contemporary political scene. This work of O'Barr's is another of the numerous unhistorical works about women in politics in Africa and Ghana. Besides, the nearest this work comes to the particular case of Ghana is its mention of Justice Annie Ruth Jiagge as "Ghana's first woman lawyer, judge and supreme court justice who is internationally active in church and legal circles". The other women whose political pedigree were clearly over and above that of Mrs. Jiagge did not receive mention. Neither did O'Barr indicate through analysis whether there had been a progression or regression. The issues that the women championed also did not receive mention.

Paul Cammack, David Pool and William Tordoff's Third World Politics: A Comparative Introduction laments over how the advent of colonial bureaucracies and the development of export-oriented colonial economies led to a marked deterioration in the role and status of women. The new leaders of Africa after independence inherited the bureaucratic and economic structures of the colonial period and thus superintended over the continual deterioration of the position of women. Readings by this researcher did not contradict the assertion of these authors. This researcher, however, went a step further to know some of the women who were able to assert themselves and the contribution they made to the development of the country.

In an article in Tsikata, Dzodzi (ed) Gender Training in Ghana: Politics, Issues and Tools, Elizabeth Akpalu provides figures on the number of women that took parliamentary seats prior to 1998. She admitted that the numbers were unjustifiably low and assigned reasons such as poor educational levels, financial problems, discriminatory attitudes and lack of support from spouses as leading to this. She, however, did not mention even a single name. Neither did she write about any issue that was discussed by any of the women. These are lapses which perhaps could not have been avoided because the import of the article was to explain the need for a policy geared towards feminine awakening.

Ifi Amadiume in Re-inventing Africa devotes a chapter to a history of the transformation of African women in politics. The author gives an overview of indigenous African women's movements. In doing that the author, "draws on the work of Cheikh Anta Diop and his theory of African matriarchy as a way of re-opening the matriarchy debate in women's studies". The author writes, "It was not the colonialists who dealt the final blow to the traditional autonomy and power of African women, however, but the elites who inherited the colonial machinery of oppression and exploitation, which they have turned against their own people". This is true of the general situation of post-colonial Africa as soon as the new elites of Africa began to control the police and military forces that had been established by the colonialists. Other analyses of the author are descriptive not only of the post-colonial era but the pre-colonial and colonial as well. The specific examples, however, are examples from the Nigerian national experience. Mention is made, for example, of the Enugu Women's Association, Abeokuta Women's Union, Mrs. Fumilayo Ransome-Kuti's Nigerian Women's Union, Federation of Nigerian Women's Societies, Federation of Muslim Women's Associations of Nigeria and Women In Nigeria among others. No mention is made of the Ghanaian experience by Amadiume. This is where the current work shows relevance. Amadiume's analysis would be placed within the Ghanaian context and the Ghanaian experience discussed on its own merit. C. K. Brown, N. K. T. Ghartey and E. K. Ekumah in Women In Local Government – A case study of Central Region write about the contributions of the National Council on Women and Development and the 31st December Women's Movement to political awareness creation and realization among women among others. The authors write that the influence of the latter overshadows that of the former and that the increase in number of women politicians in the country in the 1981-92 period is indirectly attributed to the 31st December Women's Movement. As academics in development studies, the authors could not have gone beyond the issues they discuss and mention personalities. This is one difference their work would have with the work undertaken by this researcher.

In African Women In towns: An aspect of Africa's Social Revolution, Kenneth Little gives a little description of the role of Ghanaian women in politics. He writes, "Their [women's] distinctive place in Ghanaian politics, too, involved a tie between the women's section and the party structure with horizontal links at the branch or constituency level. Thus as explicitly laid down by the CPP constitution each party branch shall have a Women's section to cater for the special interest of women, but the Women's Section shall be part and parcel of the Branch". This quotation gives an idea of the political organization of women in the First Republic of Ghana. The author does not, however, go into the specifics in terms of the names of the women who made it to government and some of the issues they dealt with. The work does not also mention, for example, whether the women spoke about affirmative action, tackled certain misconceptions about women, etc. The personal impressions of these women whether singularly or collectively were also not treated.

Amadou-Mahtar M'Bow in a contributory article to Women: From

Witch-hunt to Politics pays tribute to the fight women have put up and the suffering they have undergone in the fight for freedom and the dignity of humanity. He describes them as, "great yet unassuming figures who have waged a heroic struggle against injustice and tyranny". This is true of women when the scope is narrowed to the specific case of Ghana. What the author does not include in his write-up is the specific women who played those roles. The author does not write about trail blazers in the post-colonial life of these nations. The specific case of Ghana also does not receive mention.Deborah Pellow could not have given a better survey of the situation of women in the social system in Women In Accra: Options for Autonomy. She had this to say, "Habitually dominated by men, and excluded from high-level participation in the social system, women are usually thought to be, and indeed often believe themselves to be, inferior to men... and the men and women of the societies studied have offered us little information on the women's realm. Thus the role of women has been accorded little consequence". What the author did not see was that within the same Accra and at the same period of her research, there were women like Sophia Oboshie Doku, Mabel Dove-Danquah and Hannah Cudjoe among others who had overcome this habitual domination and the inferiority complex that went with it.

Takyiwaah Manuh in an article in Kwame Arhin (ed) The Life And Work of Kwame Nkrumah traces the role played by women in the era of Kwame Nkrumah. She begins with a sketchy overview of women in Ghanaian society and continues with their role in the anti-colonial struggle through the post-colonial nation to their role in African Unity. Mention is also made of the National Council of Ghanaian

Women. Takyiwaah Manuh's article is a brief survey. It, therefore, could not be exhaustive even in respect of that era she writes about. Nothing at all is said about the post-Nkrumah era. This research has attempted to say something about the post-Nkrumah era. Theresa Larteley Lartey has written an undergraduate dissertation entitled "Women in Ghanaian politics [1951-1990]" to the Department of History, University of Ghana, Legon. The main text of this work is a profile of three distinguished Ghanaians: Susanna Al-Hassan, Joyce Aryee and Esi Sutherland Addy. The work is a biographical sketch and speaks briefly about the involvement of the three personalities in the government of the Provisional National Defence Council. Additionally, it gives an idea of the contribution of Susanna Al-Hassan to the government of President Nkrumah. It does not attempt to treat the subject of Ghanaian women's involvement in politics through time as this work has tried to do.

Beatrix Allah-Mensah has written a book entitled Women in Politics and Public life in Ghana. The core of this work deals with women and the political process in Ghana, women in public offices and institutions and women in the public bureaucracy. It treats the period from 1992 to 2004. There is also a chapter dedicated to the use of education as a tool for enhancing the participation of women in politics and public offices. In the introduction, one finds a historical synopsis of the involvement of women in politics and public life. The treatment here is the 1956-1992 period. Essentially, this work is not historical. It is a work of political science aimed at making a quantitative survey of the participation of women in politics and public life in Ghana under the Fourth Republican dispensation.

SOURCES

A lot of the material has been primary source based. Archival materials were expected to be relied on. Enquiries at the Public Records and Archives Administration Department in Accra, however, showed the inadequacy of this source. Interviews were also conducted.

Secondary sources were altogether not sidestepped; their paucity and shortcoming notwithstanding. Published newspaper articles were heavily consulted and treated like any ordinary source. The National Gazette and the Hansard were also useful sources of historical information to the researcher.

The libraries were used. The underlisted proved to be very important:

(i)   Ghana Library Board, Accra

(ii)   George Padmore Research Library on African Affairs

(iii)   University of Cape Coast Library

(iv)   Ashanti Library, Kumasi

(v)   Balme Library, University of Ghana, Legon

(vi)   Department of History, University of Cape Coast.

REFERENCES

1. Coulter, M. Edwin, Principles of Politics and Government, 3 edition, 1987, Allyn and Bacon, Inc, Boston
2. Ibid.
3. Thiele, Leslie Paul, Thinking Politics: Perspectives in Ancient, Modern and Postmodern Political Theory, 2003,Chatham House Publishers, New York
4. Ibid
5. Magstadt, Thomas and Schotten, Peter. M. Understanding Politics: Ideas, Institutions and Issues, 1984, St, Martins Press, N. Y
6. Bluwey, Gilbert Keith, Political Science : An Introduction, Anansesem Publications, Accra, 1993 ,p i
7. Ibid
8. Ibid
9. Bluwey, Gilbert Keith, op.cit, p2
10. Bluwey, op. cit ,p. 7
11. Ibid

Chapter One

AN OVERVIEW OF THE POLITICAL POSITION OF WOMEN PRIOR TO INDEPENDENCE

GHANA AND HER PEOPLE: This survey would start with a brief description of the ethnographic and anthropological state of Ghana. A look would be taken at some of the women who within the traditional political establishment made impact on their people either as kings or queens. The ethnic groups in Ghana being either distinctively matrilineal or patrilineal, this discussion would place women in perspective in each case.

Another aspect of the history of women in politics that would be looked at and which would be in detail is the contribution of women to the independence struggle. This would be looked at in detail because of how vital this contribution was to the struggle. Secondly, it was this contribution that was to convince Dr. Kwame Nkrumah that women were capable of being able to help the men of Ghana to advance the socialist cause of progress and prosperity for the newly independent country and its people.

In writing about the political activities of Ghanaian women, it is expedient to discuss briefly Ghana and her people. This is to help erase some of the baffling ignorance occasionally exhibited both by African and non-African scholars. Two aspects of the Ghanaian people that appeal for discussion are ethnography and anthropology.

The following are the ethnic groups in Ghana: , Ewe, Ga, Gurma, the Grusi, Mole-Dagbani, Ahanta, Guan, Krobo, Ada, Akpafu, Lolobi, Likpe, Nkonya, Avatime, Logba, Tafi, Santrokofi and the largest ethnic group, the Akan. Altogether forty-nine languages are spoken in the country. This shows the extent of ethnolinguistic diversity in this small country. Another diversity, a bit less pervasive than language, is that of customs and traditions including inheritance laws and principles of political participation. It would, therefore, be incorrect to make an absolute statement about the country in respect of traditional principles of inheritance and political participation.

More relevant to this work is the different roles played by women within the different ethnic settings. Here, a broad dichotomy could be made between patrilineal Ghana on one hand and matrilineal Ghana on the other. Within the latter, women could rise to prominent political positions as queens and in rare cases chiefs. In the former, such political pre-eminence is unheard of or rare to say the least. This is the first background against which the activities of Ghanaian women in politics and government should be understood.

In understanding that, one would also have to have at the back of their mind that in the pre-independence era, as now, the relationship between women and politics or the role of women in politics has been based on the nature of the societies themselves and the changes those societies have undergone. This also means that the position of women should as much as possible be appraised within the context of the socio-political framework of those societies.

WOMEN IN PRE-INDEPENDENT TRADITIONAL SOCIETIES:

An overview of the political situation in pre-independent Ghana shows various important roles played by women in the states that existed independently of one another before the development of the country into what systematically became the Gold Coast Protectorate, colony and then the new nation Ghana.

As has already been mentioned, in the Akan or matrilineal system, women could rise to political pre-eminence. It has to be mentioned, however, that this rise was inherited rather than earned. The queen-mother appeared, more or less, to be the highest political office holder (a status that was in most cases overly ceremonial) and was seen as the mother of the chief. More often, she was his sister but the title, "hemmaa" (female monarch) was usually translated queen-mother. As part of the responsibilities of the queen-mother, she was expected to advise the chief about the way to conduct himself. According to K. A. Busia, "she may scold and reprove him in a way none of his councillors can. When a chief's stool becomes vacant it is from the queen-mother that the elders ask for a man to fill the vacant stool. As the mother of the members of the royal lineage she is regarded as the authority on the kinship relations of the lineage..."[1] Again, he writes, "Queen-mothers have their own stools, on which they pour libations and offer food and sheep on an "Adae"... The queen-mother was a member of the chief's court, and was given her share of court fines and fees."[2] The description given by Dr. Busia could be described as the constitutional and legal basis of the queen-mother's power. It was this power which invariably further gave her the authority to nominate a chief to succeed to a vacant stool.

The position of queen-mother appears to be as old as the institution of chieftaincy itself. This notwithstanding, a glance through history reveals only a handful of trailblazers whose names indelibly remain in the hall of fame of Ghana's traditional political history. These queen-mothers owed their power to the matrilineal system of property inheritance and political succession. It is, therefore, not surprising that most of the important women traditional political leaders have been from the Akan areas of Ghana.

Among the Akyem (one of the single largest sub-groups within the Akan ethnic group), the queen-mother Dokuaa who later ruled for several years as the Okyenhene [Akyem King] is the most important woman in traditional politics prior to the nation becoming independent in 1957. The Okyenhene Dokuaa, as she became popularly known, became Okyenhene in 1817 when there was no male royal of age to succeed to the throne. She became an important woman in the politics of Akyem Abuakwa in particular and the Gold Coast in general. She, for example, was one of the Gold Coast rulers whom the British and the Danes approached when Governor MacCarthy decided to have a full-scale war with Asante[3]. She travelled to Accra in 1823 to formally side with the British and the Danes against Asante.[4] One has to be reminded that Asante at this time was the most powerful nation in what is now Ghana and, therefore, needed a king with a heart full of courage to dare her. Asante's military prowess and multiple victories did not deter Okyenhene Dokuaa. With the collaboration of Okuapemhene Addo Dankwa, Dokuaa mobilized an army that in 1824 defeated the great Asante army.[5]

Kofi Affrifah cites a few instances of Okyenhene Dokuaa's role in the politics of Akyem Abuakwa and the Gold Coast. He writes, "Reindorf recalls that in the 1820s when the Kotoku arrived in Abuakwa, Okyenhene Dokuaa asked them to choose any of the following towns for settlement: Gyadam, Adasewase, Muoso, Mampong, Odubi and Asafo; the Kotoku selected Gyadam as their capital".[6] The Kotoku migration into Akyem Abuakwa was a spill-over from the numerous Asante wars with the Akyem. Affrifah's citation suggests the power that she might have wielded. Again, like the collaboration with the Danes, British and Akuapem against the Asante, Okyenhene Dokuaa's action of providing refuge to the Kotoku is indicative of the tenacity of her character. Her action also implicitly meant that the powerful Asante empire was not an ally whose friendship she needed to court. Neither was she fearful of the consequences of outwardly behaving in a way that meant resentment towards Asante.

The Kotoku were not the only anti-Asante elements Okyenhene Dokuaa accepted into her fold. She also accepted the Dwaben (Anglicised and popularly accepted as Juaben). Affrifah again writes, "...since the creation of the Asante confederation (or Union) in the second half of the seventeenth century, there had always been a muted rivalry between the states of Kumasi and Juaben. The rivalry resurfaced and intensified after the defeat of Asante in the Akatamansu War of 1826, and finally developed into an open war between the two states in June-July 1832. Kumasi forces invaded and defeated the Juaben. The latter, led by their chief, Kwasi Boaten, his brother Kofi Boateng, and their mother Oseiwa, and Oseiwa's sister, Afrakoma I, who was then the Juabenhema (Juaben queen mother), fled to Eastern Akyem to seek asylum with Okyenhene Dokuaa.... Okyenhene Dokuaa cordially welcomed them, hosted the Juaben royal family at Kyebi for sometime before she allowed them to go and settle at Saman near Osino."[7]

One can say that Okyenhene Dokuaa played the role of a provider of refuge for people who were fleeing the advancing Asante forces. The refuge provided to the Kotoku and the Juaben portray this assertion.

The period of Okyenhene Dokuaa's reign coincided with the peak of Asante expansionism. This period became virtually synonymous with wars of territorial aggrandisement. The British too were gradually entrenching their political authority on the coast and had ambitions of making incursions into Asante. Such was the milieu in which she found herself. She was not cowed into submissiveness by these incessant wars. Neither was she overwhelmed by Asante's might and their catalogue of battlefield victories.

Indeed, Okyenhene Dokuaa showed that what the men could do at the time, the women could also do and sometimes even do it better. When the elder of her twin sons, Atta Panyin, came of age, she abdicated in favour of him in 1842. Till her death in 1856, however, she continued to be the queen-mother.

Yaa Asantewaa was famous for her role in the Asante resistance to British imperialism which reached its climax with the resistance of 1900. The British felt the need to consolidate their position after they annexed Asante and brought it under their administration. To do this, they decided to depose some of the anti-British chiefly elements in Asante and replace them with people who, though not traditionally qualified, would be at the beck and call of the British colonial administration[8]. Again, the imposition of a tax of four shillings per head was a factor in the uprising.

This was a war indemnity that was levied against Asante in 1897 after their defeat at the hands of the British.[9] In the words of M'Baye Gueye and A. Adu Boahen "…the last straw that precipitated action was the demand of the British governor, Arnold Hodgson, for the Golden Stool to be sent to him so that he could sit on it. The Golden Stool was the most sacred object of the Asante, which they considered as the embodiment of the soul and a symbol of their survival as a nation. That demand, therefore, could not but touch off an instantaneous rebellion of nearly all the principal states under the leadership of the Queen of Edweso, Nana Yaa Asantewaa"[10].

Yaa Asantewaa felt the need to preserve the integrity of Asanteman by resisting at all costs any gestures that impinged on the sanctity and sovereignty of the state. Her feminine bravery is said to be without precedent in Asanteman.

Describing the events culminating in the armed confrontation, Adu Boahen writes that it was the efforts of the Asantehene Nana Bonsu and Kwaku Dua III or Agyeman Prempeh I to recapture for Asante her former glory that remotely led to the confrontation. He writes, '… once the British were really convinced of the revival of Asante power and the possibility of the occupation of Asante and Northern Ghana by the French or Germans, they decided to bring Asante under British control, either by persuasion or force. In February 1894, they offered to give the Asantehene and his chiefs liberal stipends should they agree to accept a British Resident at Kumasi. When this and subsequent appeals made through their Fante Travel Commissioner, Vroom, had failed, the British decided to use force….On the very flimsy excuse that the Asantehene had failed to pay the indemnity imposed on Asante as far back as 1874, the British arrested Prempe I, his mother, Yaa Akyaa the Asantehemaa and most of the leading divisional and wing chiefs of Asante and exiled them to Sierra Leone. The Asante did not recover from the shock that they received on the arrest of their king until some years later. They eventually broke into rebellion in 1900 led by the famous Queen of Edweso…"[11].

The Governor and his forces were attacked by the Asante war party under the leadership of Yaa Asantewaa. This compelled the Governor to seek refuge together with his forces in the fort at Kumasi. Yaa Asantewaa and her forces attacked the fort but the Governor and his men managed to escape from the fort. The Asante fought several battles with the British in the same war lasting from April through November. The Bristish overcame the Asante scare and defeated them. Together with the other Asante generals who had helped to prosecute the war, Yaa Asantewaa was arrested and sent to exile in the Seychelles Island[12].

The resistance campaign for which Yaa Asantewaa became famous could be traced to the factor that has been so widely known and accepted, that is, growing European and, for that matter, British imperialism. In the second half of the nineteenth century, the extent of colonies possessed by a nation was one of the crucial yardsticks of importance and prestige. For mainly commercial, industrial, strategic and nationalistic considerations during the last three decades of the nineteenth century, the European nations pushed further into the inland of Africa from the coast where they were engaging in their activities previously.

An interesting point worth noting is that Nana Yaa Asantewaa was not a member of the mainstream Oyoko royal family which is obliged to present a king and queen to the Asante monarchy. As a result, she was not and could never have been an Asantehemaa (Queen). This fact is mostly lost on people especially when one looks at how tall she stands in the military history of Asante. Her status appears to have toward above all known queens of Asante. Edweso, where Nana Yaa Asantewaa was queen was not one of the principal states of the Asante Union. Though it was important to the union, its chief and queen-mother were not a part of the Asante Kotoko which is the replica of a modern government's cabinet.

A lot has been researched on Yaa Asantewaa. Of all the lot, very little is known about the administrative and intellectual capabilities of Yaa Asantewaa. All what has been studied about her is her courage, tenacity of purpose and determination which made all the difference in demonstrating to the British that they could not get off lightly as far as subjugating Asante was continually made an integral part of colonial governmental policy. The lack of knowledge about her administrative and intellectual capabilities, notwithstanding, her due place in Asante and, for that matter, Ghanaian history cannot be taken away from her. It is a demonstration of this that a girls' secondary school has been established and named in Kumasi in her memory. A museum has also been named after her in her hometown of Ejisu. Among the other sub-groups within the Akan ethnic set up, very little is known about queen mothers of the stature of Okyenhene Dokuaa and Nana Yaa Asantewaa of Akyem and Asante respectively.

Traditions told orally, however, do not take from the women in those sub-groups such as the Nzema, Sehwi, Fante, Kwahu, Ahanta, Bono and Ahafo just to mention a few the contributions that have been made by them in the various wars fought in the pre-colonial and colonial era. The various forms of support given by women such as the provision of food, water and care-taking at home during the period of the execution of wars cannot be ignored if the situation is being objectively appraised. These women certainly did not occupy positions at the forefront of traditional political leadership. If it is true that the dictum "history is about great men. Without great men there would be no history" is unnecessarily aristocratic and incorrect, the little contributions made by these women have to be gathered en masse and studied on its own merit.

The constitutional guarantee of the place in traditional politics of these Akan queen-mothers who have not been epoch-makers in traditional politics has and still remains untampered with. Busia's description of the constitutional and legal source of the power of Akan queen-mothers that has been already cited holds true for these women as well. They also nominate chiefs and reprimand them. They are more or less the de jure heads of the Akan traditional political institution.

In dividing Ghana into matrilineal and patrilineal sections, the Akan group was generally said to be matrilineal. However, there are exceptions in the Akan group. For example, the Guans of present day Akuapem who are intrinsically Akan are, however, not matrilineal. They are patrilineal. These Guans can be found in two states: Aburi and Latebi (Larteh). Here too, next to nothing is known about the activities of women prior to independence.

In patrilineal Ghana, the story of the role of queen-mothers in politics prior to the nation's independence paints a picture different from that of Akanland. In the Ewe speaking parts of the country, for example, there was no position like queen or queen mother in the period prior to independence. D. E. K. Amenumey describing the political organization of the Ewes in A Handbook of Eweland Vol. I subtitled, "The Ewes of Southeastern Ghana" says the political system adopted was chieftaincy. He describes the kind of chieftaincy that was developed as, "a constitutional head."[13] He goes on to say, "The powers of the chiefs were effectively limited by the existence of councils of Elders which they had to consult on every important matter. A chief could be destooled if he violated certain traditions. Successive grades of chiefs ranging from the lineage head, the ward chief, sub chief to paramount chief conducted the administration of each state. The post of chief was hereditary … All the lineages and clans are patrilineal and though chieftaincy is hereditary, yet within the particular lineage or clan it is elective"[14]. In this citation, mention is made of the various classes of chiefs and the methods of succession which is patrilineal. Amenumey does not make mention of queens either as constituting a political institution of their own or being peers or auxiliaries of chiefs in Eweland. Also, in the very important sub-institution of the council of Elders, which purposely acts as a bulwark against dictatorship and authoritarian leadership, there is no clue as to whether women were allowed membership. One can say with a good degree of assumed correctness that as far as political power in Eweland was concerned, women were effectively cut off from the exercise of it.

The changes that came after independence and which resulted in the creation of queens and queen-mothers known as "mamaga" in Eweland could be attributed to the new realization after independence that women, even in a patrilineal system, could be organized and recognized by giving them political titles. This might have been the beginning of the subculture of queenship in Eweland.

Another area of patrilineal Ghana is northern Ghana. For the sake of simplicity, the expression northern Ghana as used here refers to that whole mass of land north of present day Brong Ahafo region and which stretches northwards to the border with Burkina Faso. These are the Northern, Upper East and Upper West regions of present day Ghana. Like Eweland, northern Ghana prior to independence had no women in traditional central government. The chieftaincy systems in parts of northern Ghana like Dagbon, Mamprusi and Gonja just to mention a few, patrilineal as it was, gave opportunity only to males to succeed to the various "skins". Outside the realm of social and economic life, women in northern Ghana were constitutionally rendered dormant. It was unthinkable for a woman to assume any of the kingship titles such as Ya Na among the Dagombas, Naaba among the Kusasi and Nayiri among the Mamprusi. Northern Ghana has been consistent in its outlook as a patriarchal society. This is because even in the era after independence when the political set up of Eweland allowed flexibility culminating in the institution of "mamagas" or queen-mothers, that part of the country remained practically irresponsive to the new wind of change that blew across the country.

No effort was made to institute queenly titles or place women within the mainstream of traditional administration. Women were consistently thought of and treated as beings that should be essentially apolitical. Their perception of women in this light cannot be regarded as a setback to development. It has been argued that probably it is due to the way the people had been socialized over the years to accept sexual division of domestic chores and politics. It was, therefore, against the normal flow of socio-political development when in the years following independence, the first woman minister of state in the government of the new nation turned out to be a native of this part of the country.

The last section of patrilineal Ghana is Ga-Adangbeland. The identifiable sub-groups within this ethnic group are the Ga, Krobo, Ada and Shai or Adangbe. Women have generally played a very important direct part in the political history of this ethnic group. In all the other patrilineal ethnic groups and sub-groups mentioned, women have been treated and recognized as being essentially outside of the political framework. That is generally true of the Ga-Adangbe as well. Most of the traditions about them say little about women being seen on the political scene. A notable exception is a queen of Ga known as Dede Akai. Dede Akai was believed to have sidestepped the patrilineal convention and acceded to the throne as a monarch. The exact date of her reign is not known but it is believed to have been before the nineteenth century. Because her accession was against convention, she felt insecure and in a bid to entrench herself issued a number of decrees to the people. Some of these decrees portrayed her to the people as a very wicked woman. She, for instance, was said to have decreed that all old men in Ga and Awutu should be killed.

It was believed that she took this decision in a bid to rid her monarchy of people who might offer counsel to people especially to those who disagreed with her. One of the clans known as Kpakpatsɛwe did not kill their old man and hid him at a place where they occasionally went to listen to his advice and direction. Dede Akai then gave the people such a difficult assignment that the people did not know how to tackle it. The hidden old man advised them to ask her for a demonstration of the task which she failed. She was amazed at their request but was soon to realize that it was the hidden old man who was the originator of that request. This was believed to have impacted so much on her that she recognized the indispensability of elderly counsel. This culminated in her instituting what became known as "Akwashon", that is, Council of Elders in Galand. According to the tradition because the hidden old man was from Kpakpatsɛwe, the leader of the Akwashon was always taken from that clan. The six other clans also nominated a man each to serve on the Akwashon.[15]

Dede Akai was said to have met her untimely death when she gave one of her usual difficult assignments. This time, she told the people to dig a very deep pit. The people did it and at a point plotted to kill her. They asked her to come and inspect it and when she did, they pushed her into the pit and buried her alive.[16] That was the end of the political leadership of Dede Akai about whom so much is said as far as cruel leadership is concerned.

It is striking that the only woman with whom traditional leadership is associated prior to independence in Galand epitomises wickedness. This is very much unlike Dokuaa of Akyem and Yaa Asantewaa of Asante about whom so much is said in terms of bravery and ardour.

Yaa Asantewaa closed the chapter on epoch-making women traditional leaders in the period before independence. After her arrest in 1901 traditional women leaders seemed to have effectively gone into oblivion. It would be unfair to ignore the fact that the annexation of Asante following the suppression of the Yaa Asantewaa – led resistance dealt an everlasting blow to indigenous resistance to colonialism. The big chiefdoms all became vulnerable to British imperialism and appeared to be physically and psychologically incapacitated.

GHANAIAN WOMEN IN THE INDEPENDENCE MOVEMENT:

After the Second World War, the political landscape of most colonial territories began to change. A number of reasons explain this change. After the war, the colonial powers became physically and psychologically weak. This left them with little physical and psychological strength to resist any strong demands by the colonial territories[17]. The formal pronouncement of the principles of the Atlantic Charter which included self-government for all subject peoples and their right to choose the form of government suitable to them imbued in the colonies the ideals of freedom and social justice on a scale that was clearly unprecedented. Another reason for the change was the people's insatiable demands for economic and social changes. The combination of all these culminated in the formation in Ghana in 1947 of the United Gold Coast Convention (U.G.C.C.) and the breakaway in 1949 of the Convention Peoples Party (C.P.P.) [18]. This situation set the tone for political mass mobilization on all fronts. The CPP, as it turned out, was the more successful of the two in its mobilization efforts. It appealed to the general mass of the population better than the UGCC which was adjudged elitist in outlook and appeared comparatively uncreative in organization. The CPP consequently became the party that won independence for the country.

The post-World War II political economy with its import licensing discrimination and quota administration acted to produce simmering tension both in the rural and urban areas. The situation was that commercial activities came to be controlled not by Ghanaians but by foreigners[19]. Like their male counterparts, women became disgruntled with the situation. According to Adu Boahen "Another practice which antagonized the petty traders, and the Makola market women in particular, was the introduction of conditional sales by which they were forced by the European and Syrian firms to buy some goods they did not want before being given those that they really needed. Irritation continued to grow until it finally exploded in the form of the boycotting and looting of imported goods in February 1948"[20]. With this state of dissatisfaction, one would expect that any mass movement that sprang up and expressed the desire to address the issue would attract women to its fold. This was exactly what the UGCC and the CPP tried to exploit.

The CPP benefited from the moral as well as material support of women more than did the UGCC. The elitist nature of the UGCC viewed against the high rate of illiteracy especially among women, as it were, ostracized women. The outwardly classless nature of the CPP, on the other hand, became its trump card which it utilized effectively. An important point to behold is that Dr. Nkrumah, the major architect behind the formation of the CPP, realized that if the fight for independence was to be successful, it had to have mass support; especially the support of women. Consequently, each branch of the CPP was to have a section that was solely responsible for organizing and convincing women to share in the ideals of the party. A contemporary author's brief description of the organization of women in the CPP is worth quoting "Their [women's] distinctive place in Ghanaian politics, too, involved a tie between the women's section and the party structure with horizontal links at the Branch or constituency level.

Thus, as explicitly laid down by the CPP constitution, 'each party branch shall have a Women's Section to cater for the special interest of women, but the Women's Section shall be part and parcel of the Branch. There shall be only one Executive Committee for each Branch including the Women Section. The same applies to the Ward and Constituencies" [21]. The idea of a women's section within the broader spectrum of the general body of the CPP could be interpreted to be reflective of Nkrumah's belief that "the degree of a country's revolutionary awareness may be measured by the political maturity of its women." [22]

This belief invariably pushed him into, as it were, emphasizing the primacy of women in the struggle. One would definitely say that his effort at mobilizing women was to ensure the success of the revolution. The organisational resourcefulness, enthusiasm and capacity for sacrifice of a lot of women at the time of the struggle, came in handy. Few names have been identified and accorded recognition albeit small. These are the women that were so energetic and enthusiastic and had the opportunity of interacting with Dr. Nkrumah. The mass of the women, however, who were poor, illiterate and uninfluential and yet provided the physical and emotional impetus to the struggle have over the years gone without notice and acknowledgement. Nkrumah, however, made a brief but fantastic and bold admission when he wrote, "much of the success of the CPP has been due to the efforts of women members. From the very beginning women have been the chief field organizers. They have travelled through innumerable towns and villages in the role of propaganda secretaries and have been responsible for the most part in bringing about the solidarity and cohesion of the party" [23.]

Some of the women engaged in the serving of water at rallies as their contribution to the party. Some of them sponsored rallies at which policies of the CPP were explained to the masses. Also, others engaged in the collection of monies to fund the activities of the party[24]. According to Takyiwah Manuh, "some of the female members showed initiative and the Asikasu branch of the women's section, for example, organized a singing band which performed at its rallies... The women combined a variety of methods, both traditional and novel, to rally support for the CPP and drew heavily on the historical experience of Ghanaian women. Thus, at a CPP rally at Dzodze, Nkrumah was received by women in Party colours who fired guns and danced in front of the cars" [25].

The women saw prospects of good livelihood in independence. The hope of ending colonial rule and the creation of better conditions of living were enough incentives to the women. Promises of good drinking water, increase in the number of schools and health facilities, among others, were some of the promises that might have done the convincing. C.L.R. James sums up the importance of these women and the workers to the independence revolution when he writes, "In the struggle for independence one market-woman in Accra, and there were fifteen thousand of them, were worth any dozen Achimota graduates. The graduates, the highly educated ones, were either hostile to Nkrumah and his party or stood aside. The social forces that made the revolution were the workers, the market women and above all, the stratum of youth educated in primary schools who had been subjected to the influence of British university education"[26]. Indeed one market woman and additionally one unemployed illiterate woman were worth any dozen Achimota scholars. Their courage and their zeal made one wonder if they really knew precisely what the struggle was about.

If they knew, then the next question one would want to ask, rhetorical as it is, is whether independence did really fulfill their expectation. Put differently, did the ideals of the independence movement measure up squarely against the performance of the leaders when nationhood was attained? The fiery nature of the activism of some of these women provokes the question just asked. At a rally in Kumasi, one woman activist who had adopted the name Ama Nkrumah was said to have slashed her face with a razor and smeared the blood over her body in a bid to show that there was no sacrifice that she considered too great. She then threw a challenge to the men to do likewise[27].

Out of the many women who were in the mass of the CPP's following were some who were outstanding. These women rubbed shoulders with the men in the newly created political environment of the struggle. Compared with some of the men, these women were just as vocal, fearless and influential. This group of flamboyant female nationalists had among their number those whose writings or intellectual enterprises acted as a catalyst to the struggle. For instance there were Akua Asabea Ayisi and Mabel Ellen Dove-Danquah. The latter became the first African woman to be made a Member of Parliament. In the words of Takyiwah Manuh, "Women such as Mabel (Ellen) Dove Danquah and Akua Asabea Ayisi worked side by side with Nkrumah on the Evening News writing articles, demanding independence and exposing themselves to the risks attendant upon political activity in a colonial regime."'[28]

Mabel Dove Danquah was one of the pioneers of modern journalism and creative writing in Africa. Born in 1905, she entered the Annie Welsh Memorial Secondary School for girls in Freetown at the age of ten. On completion, she was sent to England where she entered the Anglican Church Convent in Bury. She then proceeded to St. Michael's college at Hurst Pierpoint near Brighton. At St. Michael's, she amazed both students and staff with her brilliance[29]. She then left for Gregg Commercial College where she took a secretarial course for four months. In 1929, she returned to Freetown and was employed as a secretary by Elder Dempster Lines, a shipping company. In 1935, she came back to join her mother and father in Accra and was employed by G. B. Ollivant. She left for A. G. Leventis where she began writing to Dr. J.B. Danquah's "Times of West Africa". J. B. Danquah was said to have described her articles as charming and this really inspired her to write.[30] She wrote about many issues particularly about men and women, and morals and manners. When J. B. Danquah's "Times of West Africa" collapsed, she wrote briefly for Nnamdi Azikiwe's African Morning Post before writing for the Daily Times of London, at that time the biggest mass-circulation paper on the West Coast. The writings of Mabel Dove Danquah shifted from the morals and manners subject to the writing of short stories for relaxation. She did this briefly before joining the staff of the Accra Evening

News in 1950. It was here that she worked with Akua Asabea Ayisi. She had to keep a low profile when many of her compatriots were arrested after the declaration of Positive Action[31]. Mabel Dove Danquah's articles and the editorial support she provided at the Evening News are worthy of special mention. Inasmuch as revolutions such as the independence struggle, as a matter of necessity, need an intellectual pulpit on which to send out the ideologies and philosophical statements, Mabel Dove Danquah must be commended for having contributed in this direction.

In 1951, she paid a visit to her aunt in Freetown, Sierra Leone. There she joined Constance Cummings–John (nee Horton) "...to work out a strategy to protest against the rising cost of living. The two women went to the market-place, ringing a large hand-bell. When the crowd gathered, they exhorted the women to a mass protest. The 20,000 women with banners, led by the(sic) Mabel and Constance, marched through the streets of Freetown, ending it all by presenting a petition to the Governor".[32] The protest yielded very positive results in the form of reduction in the prices of goods such as rice and other staple diets. The Sierra Leone Women's Movement which became renowned as a vibrant pressure group for many years owed its genesis to this Mabel and Constance–led mass protest[33].

When Mabel Dove Danquah returned to the Gold Coast some time later, she used her experience as a women's organizer in the CPP and contributed greatly to the party's political activities. She stood as a candidate in the election to the National Assembly [Parliament] that were held in June 1954 and she won beating Nii Amaa Ollenu who polled 417 votes and Imoru Mobalaji Peregrino – Braimah who polled 226 votes as against her 3331 votes[34]. Clearly, she had not only won an election but had triumphed over the gender stereotype that it was men that should be elected as representatives in parliament.

Kwame Nkrumah was very happy with the election of Mabel Dove and was reported as saying, "To my country women I say a special word. The election of your first woman member of the Legislative Assembly fills me with hope for your achievement. I trust that you will take an ever increasing interest in the conduct of our affairs." [35]

But for her phenomenal achievement of being the first African woman to be a Member of Parliament, Mabel Dove would be remembered largely for her influence as a writer. In fact, she spent more of her life as a career writer than as a political activist or politician. The first time one hears of her in active national politics is when she returned from Freetown in 1951. Her rise, however, was swift because three years later, that is in June 1954, she had gained the confidence of the CPP resulting in her nomination for the seat of the Ga Rural Electoral District which provided her with the opportunity to become the first African woman to be elected Member of Parliament. She, however, could not gain re-election in 1956.[36]

Another first that Mabel Dove chalked was the opportunity she provided (which was novel) for the other Members of Parliament who were all males to be conscious of women's issues and view them as being within the social, economic and political framework of the society, and not outside of it. "As the only woman in the Legislative Assembly, she often spoke on the need for education, social welfare and legislation to improve the condition of women and to protect womanhood. Her advocacy of women's cause succeeded in making the Assembly conscious of women's problems." [37]

Another political activist in the pre-independence period who was undoubtedly a stalwart was Sophia Oboshie Doku. Born in January 1915, Sophia Doku started school at Pakro near Nsawam before going to the Koforidua Royal School where she obtained her Standard Seven Certificate. In 1929, she entered the Krobo Girls School before entering the Aburi Teachers' Training College to train as a teacher three years later. After her training she joined the Social Welfare and Community Development Department in Accra.[38]

When the UGCC was formed in 1947, she joined it and together with Paul Tagoe and J. K. Tamakloe became the first executive members of the Accra Branch. When later in 1949 Nkrumah broke away from the UGCC to form the CPP, her deep-seated conviction in Nkrumah and his qualities as a dedicated leader of sacrifice made her decide to work alongside him. She left her job and became a clerk at the CPP office, working without pay. Later, she became one of the CPP women activists who took active part in campaigning for Positive Action [39].

After the declaration of Positive Action, the arrests of the leaders of the CPP followed. Rallies had to be organized throughout the country by Sophia Doku and her colleague women organizers notable among them being Akua Asabea Ayisi, Hannah Cudjoe and Arduah Ankrah. The leadership qualities of Sophia Doku increased with the momentum of the struggle for independence which appeared to intensify day after day. She together with Leticia Quaye, Hannah Cudjoe and Adwoa Nyabanyewan (also known as Ama Nkrumah) were appointed as Propaganda Secretaries of the CPP in 1951. In that position, she worked closely with Dr. Nkrumah, Kojo Botsio and Komla Agbeli Gbedemah in the struggles that eventually led to independence in 1957[40].

Sophia Doku's political activism and the enthusiasm she demonstrated showed itself right from the beginning. When the UGCC was founded and it appeared to be purposeful in its independence agenda, she lent it her organisational skills. Again, when the CPP was established and it appeared better focused and more visionary to achieve independence for the country, she joined it and committed herself to its organization.

A look at Sophia Doku's involvement in these parties shows a consistent and unwavering commitment to the independence cause; a commitment that ascended in pitch as the struggle gathered momentum. Patriotism was the driving force behind her energy and she continued with this sense of patriotism after the country attained independence. Her close association with Dr. Nkrumah was one advantage that provided her with the opportunity to serve the country as would be seen in her activities and contribution to the government of the First Republic.

Hannah Esi Badu Cudjoe was the main organizer of the first ever political party demonstration by women in the country. This was after the 28th February 1949 Christiansborg crossroad shouting incident. The events leading to that tragic incident that claimed the lives of three ex-service men are well-known and popularly documented elsewhere and would, therefore, not receive explanation here.

However, it would be mentioned here that it was part of the catalogue of events that acted as a catalyst to incite Ghanaians against the last phase of colonialism. Hannah Cudjoe was born at Tarkwa in 1981. She was educated at the Busua Methodist School and later at Sekondi all in the Western region of Ghana. She trained as a seamstress when she completed Standard Seven. After the failure of a marriage to J. C. Cudjoe, she went to stay with her brother, E.K. Dadson who was an activist of the Tarkwa branch of the UGCC. She was said to be running political errands for her brother even though she personally believed that politics was the preserve of men.[41]

Hannah Cudjoe had this to say about how she entered into politics, "I was a seamstress in Tarkwa with my brother E. K. Dadson who was a leading figure in the Tarkwa branch of the UGCC. Somewhere in June 1947, we received a charming gentleman who was introduced to me by my brother as Kwame Nkrumah to address various meetings of the local UGCC branch in town. In the evenings a number of people came to hold meetings in my uncle's house. One day, as they came back and I was serving Nkrumah, he asked me why I have not been attending the UGCC meetings in town. I was amazed by his question and I honestly told him I thought politics was only men's business. For the next twenty or so minutes, Kwame Nkrumah explained to me all they were doing and the importance for everybody, especially women, to get involved. By the time Nkrumah left us back to Accra, my interest was aroused in politics."[42]

Hannah Cudjoe did not enter into politics as an also-ran or merely to make up the numbers. She really was set and meant to make an impact. As she herself said, she took to explaining issues to her colleagues at work. She used to speak in trains whenever she was travelling about the need for people from all walks of life to join in the fight for self-government.

When the declaration of Positive Action resulted in the arrest of leading members of the independence movement known as the Big Six, she led a group of women to raise money for their defence. This was against an order that there was not to be any public meeting. She mobilized hundreds of people to sign a petition calling for their release. She was at the same time mobilizing women for the first ever Gold Coast women political demonstration for which so much credit is given her.

The boldness of the women, particularly Hannah Cudjoe is worthy of mention here. They marched to the District Commissioner after having smeared themselves with clay and presented their petition. Thereafter, they answered questions from the District Commissioner.[43]

Hannah Cudjoe was said to have participated in all the meetings and conferences of the Central Youth Organisation of the UGCC. She was the only woman who sat among the ten men at the meeting of the CYO held at Tarkwa in May 1949. It was at this meeting that a firm decision was taken to establish the CPP. When, as a result of this meeting, the CPP was founded in June 1949, she devoted her energy to mobilizing people, collecting money and cooking whenever the group met.[44]

Hannah Cudjoe was involved in all aspects of party propaganda including the popularisation of political songs which for a long time remained hits. She was also involved in the creation and popularisation of party slogans. When in 1951, the CPP won the first ever general elections organized in the country, she was appointed as one of the Propaganda Secretaries. She saw this as an additional responsibility since it called for the organization of women into the CPP's Women Section and the men into the Youth League. She spoke at the inauguration of numerous branches of the CPP's Women's Section.[45]

Hannah Cudjoe was convinced in the ideals of the independence struggle and the inherent conviction that the fruits of the struggle would be a fair and just country ruled not by a team of expatriate exploiters but by its own sons. Beyond that, she was convinced of the unique place women had in the new nation and the need to organize women to undertake social work throughout the country. These two convictions of hers did not end with the attainment of independence. Her failing health notwithstanding, she showed a lot of energy, selflessness and tenacity of purpose when independence was attained and people with those qualities were needed to build the new nation.

The story of the involvement of women in the independence struggle would not be complete if mention is not made of Leticia Quaye and Arduah Ankrah who like Hannah Cudjoe, Sophia Doku and Mabel Dove worked side by side with the men to bring about independence. It is true to say that the input of women (both the mass of traders, workers, farmers and unemployed and the famous women like Hannah Cudjoe,

Sophia Doku, etc) to the overall realization of independence was in all respects great. The moral support of the unidentifiable masses, the money of the women financiers and the services rendered in the form of provision of food, serving of water at rallies, composition of revolutionary songs and the whipping up of enthusiasm among a hitherto predominantly apolitical feminine population to a significant extent accounts for the success of the Convention Peoples Party which by 1949 had positioned itself to take advantage of all forms of exuberance and enthusiasm pouring out of the new wind of nationalism that was blowing all over colonial territories.

END NOTES

1. Busia, K. A., The position of the chief in the modern political system of Ashanti, Oxford University Press, London, 1951, pp 19-20
2. Ibid
3. Kofi Affrifah, The Akyem Factor in Ghana's History, Ghana Universities Press, 2000, Accra, pp.115-142.
4. Ibid
5. Ibid
6. Ibid
7. Ibid
8. M. Baye Gueye and A. Adu Boahen, article in The UNESCO General History of Africa Vol. VII, Heinemann Educational Books Ltd, 1985, London, p.143
9. ibid
10. ibid
11. Adu Boahen, Ghana: Evolution and Change In the Nineteenth and Twentieth Centuries, Sankofa Educational Publishers, 2000, Accra, pp.73-74
12. Ibid
13. Agbodeka Francis (ed), A Handbook of Eweland Vol. I., Woeli Publishing Services, 1997, Accra, pp.17-18
14. Ibid
15. Mrs. Cecilia Kotey, Lecturer in Ga, Department of Ghanaian Languages, U. C. C., Cape Coast.
16. Ibid
17. Adu Boahen, op cit, pp.149-151
18. Ibid
19. Ibid
20. Ibid
21. Kenneth Little, African Women in Towns: An Aspect of Africa's Social Revolution, 1973, C.U.P, New York, page 70
22. Arhin, Kwame (ed) The Life and Work of Kwame Nkrumah., 1991, Sedco Publishing, Accra, p.108
23. Arhin, Kwame, op.cit, page 113
24. Arhin, Kwame, op.cit, p.114
25. Ibid
26. Vieta, Kojo, Flagbearers of Ghana, 2000, ENA Publications, Accra, p.126
27. Arhin, Kwame, op.cit. , p.113
28. ibid

29. Vieta, Kojo, op.cit., pp.117-120
30. Ibid
31. Ibid
32. Ibid
33. Ibid
34. Ibid
35. Ibid
36. Ibid
37. Ibid
38. Vieta, Kojo, op.cit. pp.126-129.
39. Ibid
40. Ibid
41. Ibid
42. Vieta, Kojo, op.cit.,
43. Ibid
44. Ibid
45. Ibid

Chapter Two

WOMEN IN PARLIAMENT (1957-81)

This chapter discusses the activities of women Members of Parliament in the parliaments of the First, Second and Third Republics. Attention is not so much on the individual women as on the kind of issues they interested themselves in, the force of their conviction and the support or otherwise which they received from their male colleagues. Some of the challenges they faced which either weakened or strengthened them are also discussed.

The colourful contribution of women to the independence struggle as it were, was a clear demonstration of the political maturity of the Ghanaian woman. This was in spite of low education, poverty and inferiority complex coupled with the stereotypical conception that politics was a male preserve. One factor that outweighed all these debilitating negatives against women was the recognition which the leaders of the Convention Peoples Party, notably Dr. Kwame Nkrumah, gave to women. As was hinted in the previous chapter, Nkrumah saw the direct involvement of women as being a determinant factor in the success of the independence revolution. In his view, the political consciousness of women was a mark of the success of the revolution. One would, therefore, expect that with independence gained, the political appointments that would be made would immediately take cognizance of the role women had played and make them beneficiaries of the spoils of political independence. This, sadly to say, was not the case because as soon as independence was won, women were virtually left behind. This was the situation for at least the first three years of the post-colonial political life of the country.

The attainment of independence came with the election of representatives into parliament. In the first parliament of independent Ghana, there was no woman member. The failure of Mabel Dove Danquah to gain re-election in 1956 effectively killed what some might have hoped was going to be a progressive continuum.

Various women's organizations, some of which had been established prior to independence, however, flourished. Tawia Adamafio describes these numerous women's organizations in the country as, "a thousand-and-one benevolent societies scattered all over the country wasting our womanhood"[1]. The National Federation of Gold Coast Women led by Dr. Evelyn Amarteifio and the Ghana Women's League led by Hannah Cudjoe were the two largest of the numerous women's organizations in the country. In addition to these two were the Young Women's Christian Association and the Convention People's Party Bureau of Women Organisation. All these bodies were involved in social works and the organization and education of women[2]. About the role of some of these women's groups, particularly the League and the Federation, Edzodzinam Tsikata has observed, "In addition to talks and demonstrations on nutrition, childcare, and the distribution of clothes to needy children, the League was involved in explaining government policies. In 1960, for example, its census education unit undertook a ten-day tour of the Northern Region to explain the purpose of the Government's proposed population census. It also adopted resolutions supporting the government's proposals to turn the country into a Republic[3].

"The Federation on its part carried out a house-to-house educational campaign on the government's census in areas in the Central Region. A women's column in the Convention People's Party paper, Evening News, under the pseudonym Akosua Dzatsui supported these activities with articles discussing government policies and attacking opponents of the party and government. However, it did not have many articles on women's problems[4]".

The continual neglect of women even in the midst of the liveliness of some of these women's organizations is demonstrative of a sharp return to the political economy of the colonial period. As Paul Cammack and others have observed, "The advent of colonial bureaucracies and the development of export-oriented colonial economies led... to a marked deterioration in the role and status of women in non-Muslim African Societies"[5]. The new leaders of Africa after independence did not inherit a system that was different from the colonial bureaucracies mentioned above. It was, therefore, to be that if the new leadership did not change the bureaucratic and economic structures of the colonial period (which was almost impossible in the short and medium terms), the position of women would continue to deteriorate. Viewed from another perspective, if the new class of political leaders did not make a conscious and systematic effort to address the issue of the non-involvement of women in frontline politics, the position of women would continue to deteriorate.

WOMEN IN THE FIRST REPUBLICAN PARLIAMENT:

Dr. Nkrumah was conscious of the fact that if women were left behind, it might have an adverse effect on the life of the new nation. The Electoral Provisions Ordinance of 1953 was the legal power behind all the general elections organized in the country after 1953. There was no provision in this ordinance for affirmative action. The natural result of this was that no woman was able to gain election into parliament in the 1956 general elections. In 1959, the Representation of the People (Women Members) Act was passed[6]. This Act made special provision for the election of women as members of the National Assembly. Ten women members were to be elected as additional members of the National Assembly and were to have the same privileges, rights and conditions of service as any other member who gained their election via the Electoral Provisions Ordinance of 1953. Their elections were to be carried out by a Women's Electoral College and they could do this either in a special election or concurrently with the general election[7]. A new law was enacted in 1960 because the 1959 law was never invoked and, therefore, never came into operation. The 1960 legislation repealed the 1959 Act and provided for a different method of election of women members[8]. The new method provided that the women to be elected should represent the administrative regions in the country. The elections that were held under this Act was in June 1960 and the following women got elected: Comfort Asamoah representing Ashanti

Region, Sophia Doku and Mary Koranteng representing the Eastern Region, Regina Asamany for Volta Region, Susanna Al-Hassan, Victoria Nyarku and Ayanori Bukari for the Northern Region, Grace Ayensu and Christiana Wilmot for Western Region and Lucy Anin for Brong Ahafo Region[9].

The election of these women marked a watershed in the political history of this country for two reasons. One was that this was the second time that women had been elected into parliament; the first instance being Mabel Dove's ground breaking election in 1954 which in all respects blazed the trail not only in Ghana but the whole of Africa. Secondly, this was the first time in the history of the nation as a full-fledged republic that women had been elected to parliament and this had happened in the elections of parliamentarians to the first session of the first parliament of the First Republic .The significance of this was that women were going to be made an integral part of the legislative and administrative machinery of the new republic.

The system of government which the constitution of the First Republic set out provided that all ministerial appointments (including both substantive ministers and ministerial secretaries) were to be made from among Members of Parliament. Thus the only path that one could chart towards a ministerial nomination was through an election as a Member of Parliament. The President, according to the constitution, was the only member of the cabinet who was not a Member of Parliament and yet even the President was an ex-officio member of Parliament. Parliament was, therefore, empowered as the legislative and administrative powerhouse of the new republic.

Sandra Pepera's observation of the role of women, particularly her description of the representation of the People (Women Members) Act of 1959 and 1960 is worth quoting, "Nkrumah, the master party organizer that he was, understood intimately the need to draw women into the Convention People's Party (CPP), and advocated a role for them as vanguard activists, and even in the clumsy and undemocratic attempt to ensure women's representation in parliament (the Representation of the People (Women Members) Acts of 1959, and 1960), showed a genuine commitment to propelling women onto the national political stage" [10.] Sandra Pepera's description of the Acts as undemocratic was not different from the sentiments expressed by the members of the opposition who described it as unconstitutional. Despite their vocal stance and their condemnation of it, they failed to address the issue of how to overcome the obstacles that stood in the way of women and which prevented them from successfully competing for seats in the Assembly in the regular democratic way[11].

On the day that the ten women took their seats in the first session of the first parliament of the First Republic of Ghana in July 1960, an opposition Member of Parliament for Agona Kwabre, Victor Owusu (who later in 1979 became the Popular Front Party presidential candidate in the elections of that year), referred to the women, in his comment on the Presidential Sessional address, as "a sprinkling of 'lip-sticked' and 'pan-caked' faces of doubtful utility to the deliberations of the House" [12]. This attracted a sharp rebuttal from members on the government's side. Victor Owusu then said he intended the expressions "lip-sticked" and "pan-caked" to be compliments rather than remarks that should be considered derogatory. He, however, withdrew his words since in his view his utterance had unintentionally discomfited members of the House.

Though Victor Owusu later apologized for this remark, it did show that there were some elements in the House who had either not come to terms with sexual equality in respect of female participation in contemporary national politics due perhaps to chauvinism or male unpreparedness to sacrifice what in their view was proper democracy on the altar of affirmative action.

The new members, however, overcame this uneasy baptism of fire by Victor Owusu and made their contributions to the House on issues of both national and international interest. For example, Regina Asamany, the Convention People's Party member from the Volta Region's comment on President Kwame Nkrumah's Presidential Sessional Address to Parliament in July 1961 is worth quoting, "No nation can progress without money and manpower, and fortunately for Ghana, we have both these assets. We all know that Ghana is one of the richest spots in Africa. We have our gold, diamond, manganese ore, timber, cocoa and other products, too plentiful to mention ... can we all say today that we are making good use of our available manpower? The answer is definitely "No". This is the reason why productivity is poor. Not many people are making use of the soil, because most of our young men would not take to agriculture. Apart from the waste of manpower, there is waste of money at all levels" [14]. Commenting further on an assertion by Dr. Nkrumah in the same Sessional Address that the newly formed European Common Market was a threat to the economic survival and independence of Africa, Regina Asamany again had this to say, "It is interesting to note the attitude of the Nigerian Government on Britain's proposal to join the common Market. This is the time for all our African leaders to take positive steps to form an African Common Market. We are happy Nigeria sees with us. If our African leaders take a positive stand on this they will surely and very quickly industrialise Africa. We want industries- we want factories which can produce things from our raw materials for the European countries also to buy. Why should Africa produce the raw materials which are manufactured and then later resold to us? The Common Market has been rightly described by Osagyefo as an arm of "neo-colonialism" and we must hate it even more than we hate actual colonialism"[15]. Within these two brief citations one could see an attempt by Regina Asamany to highlight some of the critical issues of the time.

It is worth mentioning that these issues were the very issues that remained unresolved and which manifested themselves in a variety of ways by the close of the twentieth century (about forty years after being raised and discussed on the floor of Parliament). She distinguished herself in debates in the first parliament of the First Republic. This was probably what might have earned her an appointment as a Deputy Minister of Social Welfare and Community Development.

In a contributory debate on the floor of parliament, another woman, Christiana Wilmot, had this to say, "On African Unity, I feel there is no need for me to dwell at length. We are all well aware of the new Free Trade Area which we have recently established by the removal of customs barriers between us and our brothers in the Upper Volta [now Baurkina Faso]" [16]. This was part of a contribution she made in July 1961 after President Nkrumah had made the first known major move at economic integration in the West African sub-region by establishing a Free Trade Area with Bourkina Faso. She dwelt on the advantages of this move whilst drawing the attention of Ghanaians to the swiftness of the negotiations that finally culminated in the signing of the agreement. She did this by comparing the agreement with the Rome Treaty establishing the European Economic Community, "It took some three years of negotiations to agree on the Rome Treaty which was signed by the six European countries to promote their own economy. It took also that length of time to complete negotiations for the establishment of the European Free Trade Association comprising the seven. But in our case the whole exercise was completed within a period of one month. This proves that in spite of the plots of the colonial powers, there is goodwill and inspiration on the part of all African countries to unite, and with perseverance and the spirit of co-operation our final goal will soon be achieved" [17]. She cautioned against the destruction of the sovereignty of the newly independent African states, "...I am sure my colleagues will agree with me that it is imperative that our Government should be vigilant and should be on their guard to expose any of these underlying plots against the newly won political freedom of African states"[18].

Susanna Al-Hassan, cannot be left out in any appraisal of the women in the Parliament of the First Republic and their contribution to debates. She, like her female contemporaries, stunned the nation with her appreciation of national and international issues. She devoted herself more especially to issues of welfare including health and education. In a contribution to debate on the 1961 budget submitted to the House for its consideration and approval, she called for the regular visit of doctors to conduct examination on school children. This was because in her view, a lot of Ghanaian children of school going age, "suffer a great deal because their parents do not notice their illness very quickly and they keep on being absent from school and this does not make for satisfactory progress at school" [19]. Continuing on another occasion, she noted that the salary of the doctors and nurses was insufficient in its ability to motivate them to give the best services they could afford, "One point I raised last time in this House... was about the salaries of doctors and nurses. I want to take this opportunity to stress this point once again. Although the salaries of the doctors in this country have recently been increased, I think the increases are not enough. At the moment we have a number of expatriate doctors working in our hospitals and no one doubts the fact that they are doing very good work; ... when one compares their salaries with those of our Ghanaian doctors, one will see that the disparity between the two salary scales is too great. In fact, this disparity is so great that it tends to discourage our Ghanaian doctors.

I am therefore suggesting that further increases in the salaries of our Ghanaian doctors should be made so as to encourage them to give of their best" [20]. She was later appointed Deputy Minister of Social Welfare and Community Development by Dr. Nkrumah as a result of her advocacy in parliament. By her appointment she became the first woman to hold a ministerial position in the history of the country. She really did prove herself worthy to the task and was to be an inspiration not only to people outside parliament but her colleagues in parliament too. Her appointment as a minister did not result in her relegation of her advocacy role in parliament to the background. She still continued to be at the forefront of the fight for social justice and equality in respect of the distribution of the resources of the state and also in terms of the wages and salaries that accrued to workers as a result of the services rendered.

The discussion on the Maintenance of Children Bill in April 1963 provided yet another opportunity for the women members, who had, by this time, gained quite a lot of experience in their duties as parliamentarians, to make valuable contributions to the debate. There had earlier on been jeers, catcalls and counter-catcalls as a result of the heat generated by this debate. The uproar compelled the speaker to rebuke the House thus, "It seems that Members are paying no heed to orders from the Chair. If that continues I shall be compelled to name Members who disregard the authority of the chair. If a member has a point to raise he should stand up and I shall see to it that he gets a chance to raise his point" [21]. When Susanna Al-Hassan had the floor on this discussion she spoke at length concerning the need for parental care for children. She was of the view that the amount of care and attention that a child was given was very instrumental in whether that child would eventually become "a worthy citizen" or not[22].

The near-confusion that preceded her submission had been as a result of a section of the bill which the men felt might unnecessarily over-burden them in their fatherly responsibilities. "If we look back into our history before industrialization, we would find that there was the belief that the child had the "sunsum" or the spirit of the father in him after birth. Now, if the child has the spirit of the father, is it not a good thing for the father to be proud to maintain such a child? ... The indigenous set-up of a father before urbanization and industrialization even in places where we had matrilineal system of inheritance, was that before the child married, the father was held responsible for its every action. The father was responsible for training the child and teaching the child a trade until the child was married...why do we want to ignore the indigenous set-up today...?"[23] she said among others. The contributions made by the women showed a clear interest and concern especially on issues that affected women and children. The debate on the Maintenance of Children Bill was another opportunity that clearly demonstrated this. The women parliamentarians made contributions to this Bill in a manner that was clearly demonstrative of their genuine desire to contribute to a law that was being made whereas some male members appeared to be making fun of the debate.[24]

On this Bill, Victoria Nyarku, the Third Member from the Northern and Upper regions had this to say, "...I should like to draw the attention of members to the fact that in the past women suffered unnecessarily at the hands of men. We cannot agree that men can treat women as they like. We cannot encourage our men to do that. We cannot allow our men to have children without being responsible for them. This Bill should be supported by all, because with the eradication of these evils, the future will be bright... This Bill is welcome and it must have the support of the House[25]."

Victoria Nyarku believed that addressing the issue rather than bringing it to light for people to hear was the surest way of practically affecting the lives of these vulnerable women and children. Sophia Doku could not agree with her better; claiming that some men simply delighted in ruining the young girls. She called for Members of Parliament to help mothers to educate their young girls. She believed that the passage of the Bill was really going to make more women happy. She declared, "Today, the women of Ghana will really feel happy because some of them who have been driven away from their husbands' homes, with their children, will now be properly cared for. We all know the difficulties we have been encountering with regard to broken homes and that is the more reason why members should support this Bill.... Members are in a position to know this because most of them are compelled to maintain their nephews and nieces because of the irresponsibility of their sisters' husbands... If this Bill is passed children of Ghana will become happy because they will be well fed and will therefore have good health and be able to think well and learn hard at school and thereafter play their part in the development of the country when they grow up to be men."[26]

When she had the chance to contribute to the Bill, Grace Ayensu said, "The Bill before the House is a progressive one, and I must congratulate the Minister of Social Welfare on this timely Bill. In our dynamic society, we cannot afford to allow some unscrupulous fathers to neglect their children... Quite often when such a man first meets the woman he convinces her with sugar-coated words, saying, he would give her a refrigerator, this and that. But as soon as the woman brings forth, the irresponsible man retreats... Mothers are neglected to the extent that some have to resort to other means to enable them to be in a position to look after their children... I am quite sure that when this Bill goes to Osagyefo the President who is the father of the nation, he will no doubt be happy. It reflects the true Ghanaian spirit and it is my ardent hope that all members will support it so that every child in this country will be adequately provided for by his father."[27]

On the same Bill, Mary Koranteng, who disagreed with the impression that was being created through the debate that women were not responsible for the upkeep of their children said even in the villages, beyond the housekeeping money, men did very little at home. She, therefore, called for men to, "realize that women too are responsible for looking after the children, although it is the man who shoulders the greater part of the burden by providing the money."[28] She maintained the stance taken by the speakers that preceded her that men who had extra-marital relationships must shoulder the responsibilities that go with them especially if an issue resulted from the relationship. "Most men have what I may call registered wives and so they fear to maintain their children born outside the registered marriage. If a man knows that he has a registered wife and he does not want trouble, he should stay in his house by his wife. If he cannot control himself and goes out in the night after other young girls then he must be prepared to bear the burden of maintaining any innocent child he may have outside his registered marriage."[29] With the seriousness went the humour. An instance of humour was when in this same debate Mary Koranteng added, "Another cause of trouble is the case of a beautiful girl from a poor family. It often happens that a lawyer or an MP or some other professional man sees the girl and woos her and starts giving her plenty of money, with the result that she ceases to respect her own parents. The man, who has a wife, hires a room for her and furnishes it with radiogram, vono mattress and other things which the girl does not enjoy at home. The man takes her along on treks and gives her a car. Because the girl is not experienced, when she becomes pregnant, the man takes her to a dispenser for an abortion. When she gets an experienced friend to advise her not to cause abortion again, the man gets some people to watch her movements with the aim of getting an excuse for abandoning her. As soon as any of them sees her talking to any young man who visits her – mind you, they may even not be in bed – he reports to the man and the man says that because young men have been coming to her, he is not responsible for the conception. It is because he is afraid of his wife and because the law says that he should not have children outside his registered marriage that he now seeks to abandon the poor girl." [30]

The issue of resignation of nurses from Government Service was brought to the floor of parliament by Victoria Nyarku. She revealed statistics that were not only alarming but threatening to the sustenance of the numerous health centres, clinics and hospitals that had been opened by the government especially in the rural areas. She revealed, "During 1961 a total of 104 Nurses resigned. Out of this number 77 were trained nursing staff and 27 were pupil nurses and ward assistants. Out of the 77 trained staff who resigned, 22 did so in order to go to the United Kingdom for further studies, 20 on grounds of marriage, 20 on account of domestic problems and 13 without stated reasons."[31] She questioned the use to which the scores of new health centres and hospitals would be put in such a situation. Viewed against the backdrop of an already understaffed health delivery sector, one would accept that these numbers were startling. Lucy Anin, the Member for the Brong Ahafo Region, could not help but add her voice to the debate. She chose to dwell on the problems facing nurses in the various hospitals.

She spoke about accommodation, rampant transfers and the lack of social amenities in the rural areas especially for nurses who had had a taste of city life and had been used to telephone and pipe-borne water, for example. She cited the case of a nurse who had been transferred from Korle Bu, "Take the case of a nurse who has been transferred from Korle Bu to Kwame Danso in the Brong Ahafo Region. The place —Kwame Danso- I am talking about has no telephone and water supply facilities. First of all, this nurse will find difficulty in getting school for her children and worse still she will find difficulty to get in contact with anybody outside this town." [32] She called for an increase in the bond of trained nurses from one year to about two or three whilst calling for better conditions of service for them as well as midwives.[33]

Another instance of contribution from a female member of parliament in the first parliament of the First Republic was when a motion to place on record the House's appreciation of the West Africa Cocoa Research Institute (WACRI) now Cocoa Research Institute of Ghana (CRIG) was moved in parliament in February 1962. The Member from the Ashanti Region, Comfort Asamoah's brief but fantastic contribution to that debate is worth quoting, "I have the greatest pleasure in supporting the motion before the House. We all agree with the statements made on the excellent work being done by WACRI. Many vital experiments are carried out in this institute which are of general interest to Africa, both economically and socially. We women in Ghana are very proud of this institute since the economy of Ghana is dependent to some extent on the successful results of its experiments. Ghanaian women should also be encouraged to learn of the various scientific aspects of the institute. We must congratulate the workers of this institute and urge them to continue their useful services to the country. They must be consoled by the fact that mother Ghana is always proud of them.

I support the Motion." [34] In this brief speech, the general patriotism and appreciation of issues of national importance that cuts across all the contributions cited earlier is found here too. She proceeded further to unofficially express the happiness of Ghanaian women about the work of WACRI and its multiplier effect on the economy of the nation.

Cecilia Ayanori Bukari was the second Member from the Northern and Upper Regions. She was noted for making contributions on domestic issues and restricting herself to issues that directly affected the mass of ordinary Ghanaians. Her comments on President Kwame Nkrumah's Sessional Address to the House in July, 1961, attests in part to this. In her introductory remarks she said, "I should like to base my contribution on our domestic affairs."[35] She expressed the hope that with the government's opening of new technical institutes in the northern part of the country, more technicians would be produced to meet the country's great need for them. She spoke about the government's new tax regime and how it could affect the country's development. "We all know that with the rise of wages and salaries the cost of labour has also risen and I would therefore plead that in the matter of taxation the case of farmers may be more carefully looked into. I know that all the farmers are one and I think that all hon. Members will agree with me that when farmers in the South are affected in any way by price fluctuations or seemingly excessive taxation, our country's progressive development will be retarded" she ended.[36] When the budgetary estimates of the Ministry of health were presented in 1961 for debate, Ayamori Bukari once again took the opportunity to make a contribution. She began by commending the government for the allocation and even asked for more funds for the ministry. She then made "a special request" to the Minster of Health, "I should like the Government to put up clinics at Pusiga, Widana and Kulungu in the Upper Region. I would also call the attention of the Minister to the fact that there are not enough beds in the Bawku hospital which is really the busiest hospital in the Upper Region, for it caters for a very large area, and I would ask that it should be fully equipped to enable it to serve this large area satisfactorily." She reminded the Minster about the need for accommodation for the health workers too.[37]

It could be said that the women Members of Parliament in the first parliament of the First Republic proved themselves capable of really "going shoulder to shoulder" with the men. From all indications, not only was Dr. Nkrumah not disappointed by these women but the adventure he risked by his "undemocratic" inclusion of the women had been worthwhile. They involved themselves in all aspects of parliamentary work; asking questions, tabling bills, moving motions, seconding motions and introducing insights during debates on the floor of the House especially into the peculiar and sometimes complex issues directly or indirectly affecting womanhood. They were articulate too. Their contributions did not portray them as feminists through and through. Collectively, one could describe them as people who were essentially multi-dimensional in their appreciation of and commitment to issues that affected the nation as a whole. Sophia Doku's contribution during the second reading of the Amendment of the Criminal Code in February 1961 exemplifies such objectivity and broad-mindedness.

She denounced the western system of marriage which disregarded polygamy and blamed that system for encouraging prostitution, bearing of illegitimate children and child delinquency.[38] "A man will be responsible for the care and maintenance of all his children if he has the liberty to marry as many wives as he can. The system of one man one woman will not do...in Ghana."[39]

She added, "I am therefore asking the Minister to bring in a Bill to encourage our men to marry more than one woman. If this is done the men will feel bound to look after their children. Besides, there is bound to be competition among wives as each one will strive by her service and industry to please the husband most. Above all, prostitution will disappear from the country. I know many prominent men in this country who are compelled to leave their legal wives and children in the house in the night and go about chasing other women. For these reasons, I feel that we must encourage polygamy in Ghana and abandon entirely the western system of marriage."[40] This view, controversial as it was, reflected the opinion of a lot of her male counterparts. Her female counterparts, most of whom made contributions after her, did not either categorically or covertly disagree with her open endorsement of polygamy; a system that, has been argued, affects women more negatively than men.

An appraisal of the first parliament again reveals that debates were often done in ways that were essentially non-partisan. It was common to find Members of Parliament within the same political party, say the CPP, debating along explicitly opposite lines. Again, debates were not done on sexual lines. That is to say that there was no antagonism between the men and women necessitating the taking of entrenched positions during debates in the House. Issues that were brought to the House and that affected men more than women were debated in a manner that showed that it affected the nation and vice versa. A case in point was when during Question Time in June 1963, Mr. B. F. Kusi, Member of Parliament for Atwima-Nwabiagya asked Mr.Henry Torgbor Provencal, the Minister for Defence, "what immediate steps is the Minister taking to raise the standard of policewomen to enable them to enter the (Police) college and take part in the competitive examinations?"[41]

To this question, Mr. Provencal replied that when women reached the required standard they would be considered. Earlier, Cecilia Ayanori Bukari and Comfort Asamoah had sought to know about the position of women as far as recruitment into the officer core of the Police Service through the Police Staff College was concerned.[42]

After close of work from Parliament House in July, 1963 Regina Asamany, then the Deputy Minister of Social Welfare and Community Development had the bizarre ordeal of being beaten within the precincts of Parliament House by two women. This resulted in her presenting a personal statement on the floor of the House the following day. The leader of the House at the time, Kofi Baako, read relevant portions of the National Assembly Act, 1961, which dealt with contempt of Parliament making it clear that the Deputy Minister had the right to make a formal report to the Police simultaneously with a complaint to the National Assembly which could refer the matter to the committee of privileges for extensive hearing and investigation. The Speaker then told the House that a Member had reported to the House a breach of privilege. He then requested the opinion of the House on the matter. E.K. Dadson, Member for Wassaw South and A. Casely Hayford, Member for South Birim who made contributions on the matter expressed their sympathies to Regina Asamany. Whilst E.K Dadson felt that in view of the gravity of the situation, "a committee of privileges should be called upon to look into the matter carefully", Casely Hayford said, "we must get to the bottom of this matter to see whether it was due to new influences or circumstances within our Party-circumstances which if not carefully handled, may create a division in our party. The matter should be gone into and amicably settled". Other contributors who made submissions on the matter did not depart from the stance of the two men already cited. They were categorical in their argument that the dignity of Parliament had been impinged[43]. This is noteworthy if one considers the fact that an alternative reaction could have been that this was a matter of a scuffle between some women needless to be allowed to take the precious time of parliament.

THE FIRST REPUBLICAN CONTINUUM: The story of the feminine voices in the First Parliament of the First Republic sent home the message that they really did deserve another turn. In 1965, therefore, when the term of the First Parliament came to an end and there had to be another set of parliamentarians, women were nominated. These were: Victoria Tagoe representing Birimagya, Margaret Martei representing Asamankese, Paulina Senanu representing Wego, Serwaa Anin representing Asante Akyem, Margaret Ocran representing Amanano, Lily Appiah representing Nsawam-Aburi, Agnes Tahiru representing Chiana, Saara Adu-Gyamfi representing Jaman, Victoria Nyame representing Kintampo and Winifred Dua (nee Prempeh) representing Asakoduase. The rest were: Comfort Asamoah representing Asante Mampong, Grace Ayensu representing Gomoa, Christiana Wilmot representing Shama, Regina Asamany representing Kpandu, Lucy Anin representing Bechem, Susana Al-Hassan representing Nanton, Sophia Doku representing Ablekuma and Cecilia Ayanori Bukari-Yakubu representing Pusiga[44].

The election of these women again is very significant. In terms of the number there was a progression. This did not reflect in percentage terms because President Nkrumah increased the number of constituencies to one hundred and ninety-eight. The women no longer came to represent the administrative regions as before but represented actual geographical constituencies. Women Members of Parliament were thus no longer the cosmetic representatives that the regional representation appeared to have made them in the eyes of certain people. Their identification with constituencies meant that they had now been technically and practically made representatives of the people within a geographical area rather than representatives of a sectional or strategic interest as was formerly the case.

The increase in women parliamentarians, with the inclusion of new members, undoubtedly increased the morale of the older members. Both old and new members collectively made their mark as far as debates in the House and general parliamentary work was concerned. It is important to state here some of the contributions made by the women in what was to be the last phase of parliamentary life under the government of the First Republic. Serwaa Anin commenting on the motion to debate President Nkrumah's Sessional Address to the National Assembly in August sounded cautions, "On this my first occasion of addressing this august Assembly, I am deeply conscious of my shortcomings in relation to the procedure of this House and I can only hope that you will, Sir, extend to me your kind indulgence if I make heavy work of it all."[45] She nonetheless succeeded in exhibiting a very high level of appreciation of the issues raised in the speech. "The peace of the world is very much disturbed by the Vietnamese war" she said "and we are grateful to Osagyefo the President for the initiative he has taken towards a solution of this seemingly intractable problem. Unfortunately, the American Government's continued bombing of North Vietnam is serving as a stumbling block in the way of the efforts of the United Nations towards a final solution of the Vietnam crisis along the lines envisaged by Osagyefo the President."[46] This speech was against the backdrop of the United States' War with Vietnam which had become a concern to nations around the world and had consequently compelled President Nkrumah in his Sessional Address to make a public statement on it.

On domestic issues, Serwaa Anin had this to say, "At home, among the topics of general concern is the apparent food shortage. I use the word "apparent" advisedly because I do believe there is no real shortage of foodstuffs at all in this country. What lead to the apparent shortage of food are the poor system of distribution and transportation from the areas of production to the areas of consumption, and the greed and avarice of speculators and profiteers who persist in creating artificial shortages for the purpose of getting rich quickly."[47] She praised the government for its newly enacted law against hoarding as being in the right direction whilst calling for its enforcement to be vigorous. She, however, was quick to add, "This is not the only thing to do. Improvement to, and an increase in the number of feeder roads will help to ease the food shortage; and I suggest that voluntary labour in the rural areas should be channelled into the construction of feeder roads instead of always erecting community centres and post offices and the like.

The Minister of Finance may also consider the possibility of getting some lorries to be engaged exclusively for the transportation of foodstuffs from the farming areas and allowing the drivers of such vehicles to buy petrol at slightly cheaper rates ...." She also called for the creation of food distribution co-operatives whose functions would be to organize the distribution of foodstuffs within stated areas in order to ensure, "profiteers and speculators are entirely eliminated from the system."[48]

Victoria Nyame who was Member of Parliament for Kintampo in a debut speech in the House said she felt honoured to be in the House and to have the opportunity of associating herself with its deliberations."[49] On the increase in the number of women Members of Parliament, she saw it as, "a clear manifestation of the great confidence the Convention Peoples Party and the leader have in the potentialities of Ghanaian womanhood."[50] The occasion was debate on the Sessional Address of President Nkrumah. She went on to speak on the substantive address, "On the question of education, I congratulate our leader and the Party on the introduction of fee-free education from the primary to the University level. The need for higher education for the women of this country at this stage need not be over-emphasized. But with so many women in higher institutions in the country, it is rather pathetic to know that in the whole of the Brong-Ahafo Region, there is not a single such institution. Though I am aware that at the present stage of our socialist development we should not clamour for amenities for individual constituencies yet I find it my bounden duty to appeal to the Minster of Education to see to the earliest establishment of a women's training college and a girls' secondary school in the Brong Ahafo Region."[51] She commended President Nkrumah for the efforts he put in the dream of what had become the organization of African Unity. She was happy, "... recent developments in our efforts towards African Unity have baffled our enemies [reference to the West and former Colonial powers] so much so that they have now realized that Kwame Nkrumah of Africa never tells lies. The persistent effort with which our great leader has championed the cause of African Unity is a clear manifestation of his sincerity in African Politics. We in Ghana should be proud that in future when the history of this country comes to be written, the name of our great leader will be embossed in golden letters.[52]"

On the Sessional Address, Winifred Dua, one of the new female members of the House made a contribution.[53] She decided to address some of the issues raised in the Sessional Address.[54] She expressed her dissatisfaction with hoarding and black marketing by storekeepers and expressed the hope that the practice would cease to allow more people to enjoy goods at costs that were not overly exorbitant. "We are realistic enough to admit that the fall in world cocoa prices has reflected rather adversely on our balance of trade position and has consequently necessitated import restrictions on certain consumer goods. We must, however, have the courage to admit that the shortage of certain essential commodities would not have been so acute but for the action of certain unscrupulous middlemen... steps taken so far to solve the problem of artificial shortage of goods have not, in my view, been directed at the root; they have been, in fact, superficial. There appears to be three main pockets of unscrupulous activity at which attention should be directed"[55] she said. Early on, she had praised the government for having expressed interest in seeing that the Vietnam Crisis was brought to an end.

A discussion of the contribution of women to the debate on President Nkrumah's Sessional Address to the National Assembly in August 1965 cannot be complete without discussing the contribution of the phenomenal Regina Asamany. She spoke this time only about the then proposed "Continental African Union Government" and indeed did so at length. She likened the strides made by President Nkrumah to the legendary Christopher Columbus who discovered America amidsts extreme pessimism. "Osagyefo, like Columbus, has only one answer –[to the pessimists of African Unity who thought that Africa is too vast. There is no Lingua Franca. It is premature] sail on sail on and on to continental African Union Government"[56] About Nkrumah and his unrelenting efforts towards African Unity, she said, "This great son of Africa who is well versed in political science, has discerned that unless a Continental Union Government is established immediately for Africa, the hated relics of colonialism would compel African states to fight among themselves. Events have clearly justified him... We have to link power across the artificial frontiers of African states and we are happy to learn that bilateral agreements are being signed"[57] she concluded.

Cecilia Ayanori Bukari who had also distinguished herself in the First Parliament of the First Republic continued to distinguish herself in the Second Parliament. On a Motion debating Productive Industries in the country, Cecilia Bukari called for the establishment of a factory to process sheanuts into sheabutter, "We have a lot of sheanuts in the Northern Region and some in other parts of the country and yet we do not make good use of them. I am, therefore appealing to the Minister to set up a sheabutter factory at Pusiga where there are enough sheanuts. If the Minister considers that it will not be economical to set up a factory at Pusiga then I suggest that a powerful machine should be installed at the Bawku Vegetable Oil Mill to process the sheabutter"[58]. She also suggested that "pito" a popular and locally-brewed alcoholic drink should be industrialized and bottled as an alcoholic drink. "Many people in this country drink "pito" and they like it very much. The Minister should therefore, encourage the "pito" industry by bottling "pito" [59]. She was of the view that bottled "pito" would cost so little and yet bring so many economic benefits to the people.[60]

Paulina Senanu was also of the view that "Productive Industries" must be encouraged and helped. "I just want to make a little contribution. It has been said many times that Made-in-Ghana goods cost more. I feel that in some established industries the cost of maintaining the labour force is greater than the price expected of goods produced locally and to be able to pay the workers the goods must be sold at a higher price. In my humble opinion, therefore, if we want to get cheaper Made-in-Ghana goods, labour and production must match."[61]

Debate was permitted in the House on President Nkrumah's Dawn Broadcast of September 1965. Among the women who took part in the Debate on the Dawn Broadcast which was about creeping disunity and baseless rumour mongering and what it could do to the nation was Comfort Asamoah, Member of Parliament for Mampong. She was happy at the prevalence of relative unity in the Convention Peoples Party government and by extension the whole of the country in the formative years of the new nation. She recounted how people could show so much love for the sake of it and wondered if that golden era would ever come back. She then chastised MPs who, "appear before the President in "fugu" or "batakari", the smock, but visit their girl friends in costly suits."[62] This sent Jatoe Kaleo, Member of Parliament for Nadawli on his feet. He felt the references to the fugu and batakari were derogatory. Comfort Asamoah said that was not what she meant but apologized.[63]

Agnes Tahiru, Member of Parliament for Chiana, in contributing to a debate on the state of the Ghanaian Press expressed her full support for the press. "In talking about the press, we must consider this, that pressmen work all over the country and telecommunication matters very much in their duties. Will Members believe that there is only one telephone line which links the Upper Region and Accra? If a pressman stationed in this Region gets some news and goes to the Post Office to telephone to Accra the operator in many cases tells him that the line is out of order. This happens because there is only one line. The newsman has to wait for weeks before he can dispatch his news. I am therefore appealing to the Minister in charge of the press to see that telecommunications are improved so that pressmen may be able to dispatch news quickly"[64]. The speaker was so impressed with this brief contribution that he could not help but say, "That is a good point. Did members hear what the member for Chiana said?" [65] The need for a good telephone system came up again during the second reading of the Telecommunications (Amendment) Bill in the National Assembly in Sept. 1965. Margaret Martei, Member for Asamankese was of the view that the Telecommunication Corporation when set up should take great care of the telephone system and in particular the behaviour of telephone operators because the work of some organizations is delayed because of the inability of the department to dispatch telegrams promptly66. Dowuona-Hammond, Member of Parliament and Minister responsible for Telecommunications explained that the difficulty with the telephones was due to technical faults. He assured the member for Asamankese that the situation would be rectified. On the behaviour of telephone receptionists, he told the House, "I am happy the Member for Asamankese (Mrs. Martei) who is the General-Secretary of the National Council of Ghana Women raised a point about the behaviour of our telephone girls". He appealed to her to help educate the girls to behave courteously[67].

A Motion to debate Rural Water Supply in Ghana saw a number of the women members of Parliament associating themselves with the need to provide good quality water for the rural folk. Contributions by S. K. Tandoh, Member of Parliament for Bantama, Mahama Tampurie, Member of Parliment for Walewale and M. O. Kwatia, Member of Parliament for Koforidua, had brought to the fore the danger of leaving the rural areas behind in the nation's quest to provide good drinking water for its citizens.[68] Serwaa Anin took the opportunity to draw the attention of the House to the particular case of Agogo in the Ashanti Region. She spoke about the strategic and economic importance of Agogo that made it imperative to ensure an all year round supply of water. "This town has been of great assistance to this country in the past; and in the present it continues to play its part in the socialist reconstruction of Ghana. Agogo, Sir, boasts of a Girls' Boarding School whose achievements we look upon with pride. This town also boasts of primary and middle schools. And last but not the least, Agogo boasts of a well-established mission hospital. Yet in this town, water is an expensive commodity"[69] she said. She argued that in practical terms the perennial water shortage in Agogo was like, "adding insult to injury". She called on the authorities to, in doing something about the situation, pay attention to the particular case of Agogo[70]. When Sophia Doku spoke, she said that the impression being created that all was well with residents of the cities especially Accra as far as water supply was concerned was wrong. She drew the attention of Members to the fact that in certain parts of Accra, especially in Ward 3 [Sukura] the people were suffering as much as the rural areas. She argued that the situation be critically examined but in concluding reverted to the original motion thus, "the population of the rural areas is greater than that of the urban areas and we should try to provide in the rural areas the same amenities as are in the cities. People living in the small villages need good drinking water and everything should be done to give them good water"[71]

Mary Koranteng in a debate during the Second Reading of the Local Government (Amendment) Bill continued the rural amenities agenda. "It is a fact that the Government provides some grants to the councils (referring to district, municipal and metropolitan assemblies formerly known as local, town and city councils respectively) to enable them to provide amenities in their respective areas, but very often funds granted to local councils in the rural areas are very small. These funds are moreover channelled through the Regional Headquarters for distribution to the local councils and in most cases the rural areas are left with nothing. I am therefore suggesting to the minister to provide more roads to the rural areas because it is in these places that the farmers who have been helping in the development of this country reside, and by providing them with those amenities which are necessary for their living they will be encouraged to help the country"[72.] She said that every farmer had a role to play since the country was predominantly an agricultural country producing raw materials basically for export.

Among the women who took part in the debate on the motion to discuss the activities of the erstwhile Workers Brigade was Christiana Wilmot, Member of Parliament for Shama. The Workers Brigade was a pool of young women and men who were engaged to undertake economic ventures. This was aimed at reducing unemployment as well as providing a ready labour market for productive ventures. It was established by President Nkrumah. Christiana Wilmot expressed gratitude to the "great leader" President Nkrumah and praised the individual projects that the Brigade was working on. "At Omankope one will see that the brigaders are busily engaged on the farm trying to produce more food for the country. At Appam the Workers Brigade has a vast corn farm. The camp commandant there is a hard-working man and he can supply the Kanda Camp with about forty bags of corn a week. The brigaders on the various farms are working very hard and they should be encouraged. If the state farms and the Young Pioneers are given more equipment and money, I see no reason why such a big and useful organization like the Workers Brigade should not be encouraged in the same way[73]". She then made an appeal to the Minister of Finance to give the Workers Brigade more funds to help them in their work.

Activities at the Kumasi City Council (now Kumasi Metropolitan Assembly) came up for scrutiny on the floor of Parliament House in 1965. The issue was alleged misappropriation of funds at the council by the Chairman and other people in the top hierarchy of the council. Mary Koranteng, Member of Parliament for Akyem Swedru/Achease was the first woman Member to make a submission on the matter, "... the Kumasi City Council was formerly known to be an efficient council and people who heard me praise it are surprised that the council should be charged with misappropriation of funds. So I am asking the Minister to come out boldly to tell this House and the public exactly what irregularities were committed by the Kumasi City Council. I want the report of the committee appointed by the Government to investigate the irregularities to be published so that the new members of the council will be guided to avoid the mistakes of their predecessors"[74] On this same subject, Lucy Anin appeared emotional when she had an opportunity to make a comment, "we are living in an age where sincere thoughts are always questioned; where those who speak the truth and speak it from their hearts are always misjudged. All these things are not going to perturb me or prevent me from saying what I consider to be right. Today, it is Lucy Anin; tomorrow it could be someone else..." She blamed the difficulties of the Kumasi City Council on what she perceived to be "unjustified rivalries and dissensions in Kumasi."[75] The Kumasi City Council became a recurrent topical issue in the National Assembly with regard to expenditure on the bungalow of its chairman and some extension and renovation work on it.

For a consecutive period of three years, the purchase of the bungalow and other works on it became part of the financial estimates of the council. One interesting aspect was the approval the Minister of Local Government, Mumuni Bawumia gave to the estimates. Later events were to show that the Minister was wrongly advised by the council hence the suspicions and later the allegation that there had been misappropriation of funds. Concluding her rather long submission on the debate, Lucy Anin said, "If the financial irregularities... described have been substantiated, and if the suspension of the council was the result of personal ambition and intrigues of detractors of the council, then a committee should be set up to go into every aspect of the matter, so that people may know the truth and nothing but the naked truth."[76] She felt that there were many doubts in the statements that had been made on public platforms by important officials of the Convention Peoples Party.

The contributions made by some of the women Members of the second Parliament of the First Republic of Ghana leave no doubt that indeed they were a force to reckon with.

THE FIRST INTERREGNUM: The Convention Peoples Party government was toppled on the 24th of February 1966 by the National Liberation Council. This was a military government which had these people as members: Lt. Gen. J. A. Ankrah, J.W.K Harlley, Lt. General E. A. Kotoka, B. A. Yakubu, Colonel A. K. Ocran, J. E. O. Nunoo, Major A. A. Afrifa and A. K. Deku.[77]

This brought to an end all the democratic institutions of government that had been put in place by the Convention Peoples Party. All the efforts that had been made towards involving women in government and making them legitimate stakeholders in development were to be swept away completely. These included the Representation of the People (Women Members) Act of 1960. What happened to the political situation of women under the National Liberation Council government is part of the subject matter of another chapter.

WOMEN IN THE SECOND REPUBLICAN PARLIAMENT:

In 1969, the National Liberation Council government supervised elections and returned the country to yet another episode of parliamentary government. This was what has now become known as the Second Republic. This system of government under the Second Republic was very much akin to the Westminister system practised in Britain. The entire machinery of government including the chief executive of the land, the Prime Minister in this case, were all to be Members of Parliament. All ministers of state and their deputies were to be Members of Parliament. When nominations were opened, 580 candidates filed their nominations to contest in the 140 constituencies nationwide. Out of the number of candidates, ten were women. These were: Akua Asabea Ayisi and Deborah D. Awuah who contested for the Akropong and Nsawam-Aburi constituencies respectively in the Eastern Region. In the Central Region, Elizabeth Mensah and Agartha Ama Awuah contested for the Ekumfi and Denkyira seats respectively. Grace Afua Mensah (Krachi Constituency) and Esther Ocloo (West Dayi constituency) were the women candidates in the Volta Region. Others were: Mary Adukuma (Talensi-Nabdam), Lydia Akanbodiipo-Kugblenu (Sandema) and Catherine K. Tedam (Chiana-Paga) in the Upper Region (now Upper East Region). The only woman who contested in the Ashanti region was Adwoa Kufuor who contested for the Atwima-Amansie seat.[78]

The successful women candidates were: Catherine Katuni Tedam who won the Chiana-Paga seat for the Progress Party and Lydia Akanbodiipo-Kugblenu who stood on the ticket of the National Alliance of Liberals and won in Sandema.[79] These two became the voice of their constituencies as well as the voice and the symbol of Ghanaian womanhood in parliament. This is not to suggest that the male Members were oblivious to the needs and aspirations of women. The point is that, it is true that the peculiar situation of women and how they felt could best be appreciated and exposed by women themselves. From the word go, it was clear that the women in the parliament of the Second Republic would not be as influential as the women in the Parliaments of the First Republic. The regrettably insignificant number of seats they occupied in the House buttresses this point more than anything else. The two were, however, not left out in the deliberations of the House.

Even though they were numerically overshadowed, they were neither overwhelmed nor over-awed. Their utility to the deliberations of the House was not doubtful.

Lydia Akanbodiipo-Kugblenu's contribution to the debate on the State Housing Corporation (Ejectment) Bill in March 1970 is worth appreciating. She criticized the Progress Party government for not being caring enough and therefore doing very little to protect the poor from being rendered homeless,

"This Bill should not have been brought to parliament by a Welfare State Government, because it seeks to render the unfortunate lower-income group homeless, and does not give them the chance to explain the cause of their default, which may be due to loss of employment .How can the Minister expect somebody who is out of employment for a long time to be able to pay his rent regularly?"[80] She argued that since the Rent Act of 1963 provided adequate procedure for the recovery of money owed by tenants, the Bill being debated was unnecessary. This brought her into confrontation with Dr. W. G. Bruce-Konuah, the Minister of Works and Housing. Dr. Bruce-Konuah argued that the new Bill was not seeking to replace the Rent Act of 1963. The new Bill, in his view, provided that tenants who were in default for one month should be given two weeks notice and by the time the notice got to the defaulting tenants they would have stayed in the houses for two months plus the two weeks notice[81]. This was what finally settled what had generated into a two-way parliamentary confrontation for about fifteen minutes. She again was on record to have busily engaged herself in Question Time in Parliament. An instance was when she asked Dr. J.K. Fynn, the Ministerial Secretary responsible for Local Administration what steps he was taking to ease the congestion in markets and to modernize them. The Ministerial Secretary gave a lengthy explanation citing financial difficulties as one of the causes of the congestion. She then asked, "May I know from the Minister whether there is nothing his ministry can do to remedy the present situation till funds became available." The Minister of Local Administration, K. K. Anti then gave her a response, "We already have the situation well in hand. Where it is possible for us to make an improvement on a small scale we will do so. But as the hon. Lady herself will realize if she has ever visited the markets in Accra and Kumasi, the situation is such that we need a major surgery, as has been suggested in the answer" K.K. Anti then told the House plans that had been put in place to give the markets a "major surgery."[82]

Debate in the House on Northern Ghana Development in June 1970 provided an opportunity for Catherine Katuni Tedam, Member of Parliament for Chiana-Paga, herself an indigene of Northern Ghana, to make her voice heard. She said that it was obvious for certain regions in the country to draw "special attention" to themselves. This was because in her view everybody in the country was entitled to enjoy the benefits and the resources of the country.[83] About the "special attention" needed by the North, she argued "...when we look at the educational background of the North and the rural parts of the country we can see that important amenities such as school buildings, school textbooks, school furniture, playing equipment as well as accommodation for teachers, are lacking. I hope that the Government is taking a serious view of the lack of these amenities which retards the progress of education in the country, and will make provision in the coming budget to solve this serious problem facing the country's education."[84] She again took the opportunity offered by the debate to comment on health facilities in the rural areas particularly her constituency. She expressed her dissatisfaction with the paucity of health facilities such as clinics, health posts and maternity homes, "...there are too many deaths which could be prevented if these amenities are provided."[85] Her contribution touched on other sensitive needs such as shortage of good drinking water, bad road network and lack of basic commodities like sugar, milk, soap and tin fish.

"If they are there at all they are not sufficient and are therefore sold at cut-throat prices which some of the people cannot afford. I therefore appeal to the Ministry of Trade, Industries and Tourism to try to make funds available or make special arrangements whereby these essential commodities can be sent to the remotest parts of the country if possible to open branches of the Ghana National Trading Corporation in the big villages in the rural areas to serve the surrounding villages and to help the women in particular to trade in order to look after their children and families."[86] Joseph Henry Mensah, Minister for Finance and Member of Parliament for Sunyani constituency [who later became popularly known as J. H. Mensah in the Forth Republic] was so enthused by Catherine Tedam's brilliance that he congratulated her for it. He said that she had shown a grasp of the realities of the people she represented and told the House how Members of Parliament from the Progress Party were proud of her.[87]

On the same debate just alluded to, Lydia Akanbodiipo acknowledged that the Northern and Upper Regions were lacking in everything.[88] She, therefore, called for efforts from the government to bring the standard of development in those regions to the level that pertained in the other regions of the country. She particularly spoke on the need to do something about educational standards in those regions. "May I take this opportunity to make some suggestions to the Minister of Education. We all know how bad things are in the Northern and Upper Regions. I should like to suggest that fee-free compulsory education be introduced in the Northern and Upper Regions. There was a press conference there some time ago; the Regional Education Officer said that some schools had to be closed down because they were not getting children. If the fee-free compulsory education is re-enforced we shall get some children to attend these schools."[89] She continued, "May I also say something about continuation schools which are just in their primary stages. The Ministry of Education should distribute these continuation schools evenly, and particular attention should be paid to the Northern and Upper Regions in this respect."[90] She called for training colleges particularly those in the northern part of the country to admit as many Northerners as possible.

Catherine Katuni Tedam was particularly noted for asking questions in the House. She once asked the Ministerial Secretary for Education, Sports and Culture, Sebastian K. Opon, "when girls vocational centres will be opened in the Northern and Upper Regions to train most of the girls who idle about after completing their elementary school education."[91] The Minister denied the Ministry's responsibility in the opening of vocational centres. He, however, said a technical institute at Tamale was available and all subjects taught at vocational centres were taught there. She further asked, "will the Minster consider opening one as soon as possible?"[92] Before the Minister could finish answering this second question, a third one was ready for him, "will the Minister make it possible for girls to be admitted to the technical schools in the next academic year, since at the moment there are no girls there?"[93]

To all these questions, Sebastian K. Opon replied "Yes, we will consider the matter."[94] Shortly, she asked the Minister a fourth question when she sought to know when middle schools would be built to serve the primary schools in Paga-Buru, Kuliyao, Sakaa and Kazugu, since the two middle schools in Paga could not accommodate all the pupils who passed out of the primary schools.[95] The answer from the Minister that his Ministry had taken note of the question and was studying the situation to enable it to determine what steps would be taken[96] was not satisfactory for her. She then asked a fifth question, "How soon will it be."[97] To that, the minister answered, "As soon as possible." [98]

The need to prosecute the feminine agenda was not lost on Lydia Akanbodiipo and Catherine Tedam. In a contribution to the second reading of the Ghanaian Business (Promotion) Bill, the latter drew the attention of the House to the role of women in ensuring that goods produced arrived at their intended destination. "There is no doubt Mr. Speaker that the women of this country have made a very substantial contribution to the economy of our country. They have provided the main link between the wholesale traders and the consumers even in the remotest parts of this country.

I think this House will recognize the role of the market women, for without their efforts producers as well as consumers will suffer. Mr. Speaker, if Ghana should be progressive then the women of Ghana should be taken into consideration". She said the women were determined to move into the various sectors of the economy and therefore they should be given the chance to do so. She implored the Minister of Finance to consider special measures to support the endeavours of Ghanaian women to take active part in the promotion of Ghanaian business. She also suggested to the Minister that a woman should be included in the membership of the Committee."[99]

A further demonstration of the prosecution of the feminine agenda was Lydia Akanbodiipo's reaction to a contribution by Nana Toa Akwatia II, Member of Parliament for Densuagya, that female teachers should be given three months full salary when they were going on maternity leave and that abortion was widely caused by female teachers. She argued, "...why three months? Full pay should be given to all women engaged in the public services who go on maternity leave. It is difficult to see why the hon. Member thinks that female teachers cause abortion because of lack of money... I am a Member of Parliament for Sandema and women's representative in this House. It is difficult to get the hon. Member's reason for suggesting that abortion cases are predominant among female teachers and not among female workers generally. One has to reconsider the real cause instead of attributing it to purely monetary conditions. It can be due to illness and some other conditions. At this juncture, I should like to suggest that married men should stop having illicit dealings with unmarried girls. Mr. Speaker, I should like to repeat what I have said. Married men should stop having illicit dealings with girls other than their wives."[100]

They also got themselves embroiled, like their male counterparts, in the expected game of politicization of issues. In a contribution to the debate on the Government's Financial Policy, Catherine Tedam said, "To say that the budget statement is bad is to betray ignorance of the highest order. We want constructive thinking, not lousy utterances as we hear elsewhere or read about in cheap newspapers."[101] She was of the view that much of the contributions from the opposition had been emotional and unrealistic.[102] She blamed the woes of the country on the First Republican government whose political tradition members of the National Alliance of Liberals sought to identify themselves with. (It must be noted that the National Alliance of Liberals was the biggest opposition party in parliament at this time). "It takes only a Progress Party Minister to be able to apply such a brilliant analytical mind to problems which were created by a government which was notorious for its inefficiency and autocracy. For well over 15 years, the Prime Minister of this country (Dr. Busia) and his colleagues, some dead and some still alive, tried in vain to apply the brakes to a regime that was obviously heading towards a disaster. The irony of it all is that it is the same Dr. Busia and his Progress Party who are now saddled with the task of redeeming the country from the very maladministration he spoke gallantly against."

THE SECOND INTERREGNUM: The Second Republican government could not travel its full term as a military junta, the National Redemption Council, took over the reins of government on 13th January, 1972. This was led by Ignatius Kutu Acheampong, an army colonel at the time. Later, he became a General. The National Redemption Council later reconstituted itself to become the Supreme Military Council. On 4th

June 1979 the Supreme Military Council was also overthrown by the Armed Forces Revolutionary Council. The latter returned the country to democratic rule in September 1979. It needs to be said, however, that the Supreme Military Council had already began the process of returning the country to civilian rule before its overthrow.

Kwaku Danso-Boafo writes, "The two Ghanaian coups of 1966 and 1972 were remarkably similar in that they were staged in the absence of the heads of government. However, reaction of the people was different from that of 1966. Unlike 1966 when the military regime organized large-scale demonstrations, this time there were a few of them. This was partly due to the unexpectedness of the coup. Busia's government had a mandate to rule for four years after which another general election would be called. The argument, therefore, was that unlike 1966, a coup was, this time, unnecessary because if Ghanaians were dissatisfied with Busia, they would vote him out of power in 1974."[104] Busia himself described the coup as 'officers amenities coup' and a coup staged apparently because the Progress Party government had required army officers to pay part of their utility bills.[105]

Again, like the National Liberation Council, the Acheampong-led regime brought to a halt all the strides that had been made towards enhancing democracy and by extension allowing women to become political contributors within the democratic political system (even if not purposefully intended and officially sanctioned). To what extent the National Redemption Council "redeemed" Ghanaian women and made them role-players in the politics and governance of this country is part of the sub-theme of another chapter in this book.

THE THIRD REPUBLICAN PARLIAMENT AND WOMEN: The third attempt at parliamentary democracy saw the birth of the Third Republic in September, 1979. The 1979 constitution which provided the constitutional and legal platform for all the democratic institutions of state spelt out a system of complete separation of powers. The Executive arm of the government, headed by the president, was distinct from the Legislative and the Judiciary. Under that dispensation, therefore, Members of Parliament could not hold ministerial positions and vice versa. Dr. Hilla Limann of the Peoples National Party won the presidential elections after a second round of voting during which he defeated the Popular Front Party candidate, Victor Owusu, his major opponent.

In the elections to parliament in the Third Republic, five women won seats. These were Eunice R. Ametor-Williams (Ada Constituency), Monica Patience Atenkah (Buem Constituency), Agartha Ama Awuah (Denkyira), Dorcas Constance Commey (Asikum-Odoben Brakwa) and Elizabeth Kusi-Aidoo (Densuagya). [106] This was by far an improvement over the number of women in the previous Republic though nowhere near the situation in the First Republic. Like the women in the republics before them, the women in the Third Republican Parliament made their contributions to all aspects of parliamentary life.

As was done in the discussions on the women parliamentarians in the first two republics of Ghana, the contributions of the women parliamentarians of the Third Republic will be discussed. In a debate on farming inputs, Agartha Ama Awuah called for an end to smuggling of farm inputs outside the country after the government had used its scarce resources to import these implements. She called on the University of Science and Technology and blacksmiths to help in the production of these implements. "Since necessity is the mother of invention, I am appealing to the University of Science and Technology to take up the challenge to produce farming implements to supplement the Government's effort in importing farming inputs into the country. I also suggest that blacksmith associations should be formed in all districts and that they should be given loans to improve upon their capabilities in order to produce implements such as chisels, hoes, cutlasses and so on, to supplement the government's effort."[107]

The Member for Densuagya, Elizabeth Kusi-Aidoo in a contribution on the state of the health delivery system said, The state of affairs in the hospitals is very alarming and if nothing is done immediately our mortuaries will soon be choked up. Sometimes one cannot blame the doctors and the nurses and other medical personnel for not putting in their best. Sometimes simple basic inputs for first aid to critically sick persons are not available; surprisingly infusions like saline, dextrose et cetera are found at the Makola Market being sold for ¢150.00 per pint whilst the hospitals cannot get them.[108] Commenting on an industrial action embarked upon by doctors and other health workers, she said that they went too far since their action was at the expense of human lives.[109]

In a debate on the need for civic education among Ghanaians, Eunice R. Ametor-Williams, Member of Parliament for Ada, who moved the motion said the aim of the motion was to, "call on the House to view with concern the lack of national consciousness in the society" and to call upon all citizens to, "develop a proper attitude towards nation-building and national reconstruction."[110] She argued, "Half of this country's problems would have been solved if the citizens understood what is really happening in this country. Currently, disconcerting words are flying around in the country, and everybody is decrying the present condition of our economy and the stark hunger that is stalking almost every home and making life in general unpalatable and unsavory... Ghanaians are proving themselves to be pathetically unconscionable; nobody is taking his or her work seriously. We have become experts at lobbying for posts with little intention of helping to break the vicious circle. On the contrary we unabashedly commission ourselves to bleed to death and to gauge ourselves like flies with the already anaemic blood of the country."[111] She called for an end to the pointing of accusing fingers at people instead of people taking responsibility for their actions.

On the same issue, Agartha Ama Awuah and Dorcas Constance Commey made contributions. The latter said, "...Patriotism, courage, civic responsibility cannot be taught by shouts from rooftops; opportunities should be provided for them to be acquired in the institutions. I therefore call on the Ministry of Education to reorganize and intensify the teaching of civics in our schools ... While I appreciate the intention behind this motion I am convinced that having regard to the numerous social and economic problems facing this nation giving rise to deep-seated apathy, frustration and despondency among the people, what we need now is not the setting up of a separate institution to undertake the civic responsibilities. These organizations should be made to function efficiently. They must be reorganized, re-structured and properly motivated to undertake this national assignment."[112] She cited the Information Services Department and the Social Welfare Department as examples.

Agartha Awuah on her part blamed the economic problems of the country on laxity in all sectors of the economy. She, like Dorcas Commey, argued that patriotism was key to development, "It is my view that no amount of foreign aid can save this country unless Ghanaians change and work harder than they do now. Every able-bodied citizen should contribute his or her quota to help resuscitate our shattered economy. I would urge all political parties to inculcate some patriotism in the youth". Quoting the saying, Teach the child the way he should go, and when he grows old he would never depart from it, she said when the youth are taught to know that everything in Ghana belongs to Ghanaians they will be more determined to put in their best to build the country.[113] She called for mass education since she believed it was very essential in a developing country like Ghana.

Monica Patience Atenkah, the Member of Parliament for Buem, added her voice to debate on the Lower Volta Bridge. The issue at stake was an attempt by the government to convert the loan that was taken to execute the project into a grant as a result of an alternative project design which was used by the contractor instead of the government's recommended design. Difficulties that came to be seen with the project were therefore blamed on the alternative design. The argument was that had the government's recommended design been used, there would not have been those difficulties. "The mover of the motion stated that the awarding authorities knew from the very onset that the constructional design was faulty."[114] She said this notwithstanding, they went ahead to award the contract. As a result of the blatant lapses, therefore, she felt that the motion should be rejected. "I feel that it will just be honourable on our part to honour the agreement. Mr. Speaker, with all due respect to blind men, I would say that even a blind man will not readily open his mouth for anybody to stuff it with rubbish. As the mover of the motion rightly stated, the Lower Bridge was completed in 1964. But before the contract was awarded, certain factors were taken into account. For instance, approval of the design must have been given; the constructional ability and standing of the contractor must also have been known.[115]" She argued, therefore, that there was no point in not repaying the loan on the excuse that the project fell below expectation.

THE THIRD INTERREGNUM: The Third Republican Parliament like the ones that preceded it was not able to bring its work to a programmed end as a military insurrection led by Flt. Lt Jerry John Rawlings, a member of the erstwhile Armed Forces Revolutionary Council overthrew the government on 31st December 1981. The 'council' that was formed this time round was called Provisional National Defence Council. Once again, the constitution and all the democratic institutions of state that had been put in place were thrown overboard by the "council". For eleven years, the provisional government ruled the nation.

A survey of women's parliamentary activities in Ghana from the First through the Second to the Third Republics produces certain interesting revelations. One is the fluctuating nature of the number of women in each Republic. Whereas in the first parliament of the First Republic the figure was ten, it rose to eighteen in the second parliament of the same republic. In the Second Republic, the number was as low as two whereas in the Third Republic the number rose to five.

The fluctuations can be attributed first and foremost to the unique character of each republic. The uniqueness of the republics are explained more in terms of historical facts than in theories rooted in sociology, anthropology or political science. While President Nkrumah was firmly rooted in power by 1960 to afford to experiment with affirmative action, Prime Minister Dr. Busia had to struggle his way to the Premiership and, therefore, could not toy with the seeming luxury of affirmative action especially against the backdrop of a struggle with political opponents who were as credible, marketable and potent as he was. President Hilla Limann who superintended over the government of the Third Republic came from a similar background as Dr. Busia.

Also, while Dr. Nkrumah had a special place for women within his political philosophy of socialism and also believed that the success of the African revolution depended partly on the political consciousness of its women, the same cannot be said about the governments of the Second and Third Republics. Far from saying that women were considered irrelevant to nation building in these latter republics, it is true that the political activism of women was not deemed an integral part of the determinants of the success of the governments of the Second and Third Republics.

It can also be said that the differences in the way and manner women were treated under the republics just discussed have a lot to do with the length of time each of the republics existed. Dr. Busia and Dr. Limann, unlike Nkrumah, did not stay in power long enough to take time to strategise and consciously place women in politics in a politically male-dominated society like Ghana.

Another key factor, and perhaps the most visible of all the problems that have thwarted the efforts at involving a lot of women in parliamentary democracy, is the numerous military interventions. The National Liberation Council, the National Redemption Council, the Supreme Military Council and the Provisional National Defence Council interventions effectively destabilized not only the democratic dispensation but also destroyed the chances of more women playing roles in politics.

ENDNOTES

1. Adamafio Tawia, By Nkrumah's side, 1982, Rex Collings, London.,p.115
2. Ibid
3. Hanson Emmanuel & Ninsin Kwame (ed), The State, Development and Politics In Ghana, 1989, Codesria Book Series, London.p.78
4. Ibid
5. Cammack, Paul et al., Third World Politics: A comparative Introduction ,1988 Macmillan, London, p.185
6. Arhin Kwame (ed) The Life And Work of Kwame Nkrumah, 2000, sedco, Ghana.,p.115
7. Ibid
8. Ibid
9. Ghana Parliamentary Debates, Official Report, 18th July, 1960.
10. Ninsin A. Kwame, & F. K. Drah, Political Parties and Democracy in Ghana's Fourth Republic, Woeli Publishing Services, Accra, 1997, p.136
11. Ibid
12. Ghana Parliamentary Debates, Official Report, 18th July, 1960.
13. Ibid
14. Ghana Parliamentary Debates, Official Report, 6th July, 1961.
15. Ibid
16. Ibid
17. Ibid
18. Ibid
19. Ghana Parliamentary Debates, Official Report, 17th July, 1961.
20. Ibid
21. Ghana Parliamentary Debates, Official Report, 2nd April, 1963.
22. Ibid
23. Ibid
24. Ibid
25. Ibid
26. Ibid

27. Ibid
28. Ibid
29. Ibid
30. Ibid
31. Ghana parliamentary Debates, Official Report, 24th January, 1962.
32. Ibid
33. Ibid
34. Ghana Parliamentary Debates, Official Report, 4th February, 1962.
35. Ghana Parliamentary Debates, Official Report, 6th July, 1961.
36. Ibid
37. Ghana Parliamentary Debates, Official Report, 17th July, 1961.
38. Ghana Parliamentary Debates, Official Report, 13th February, 1961.
39. Ibid
40. Ibid
41. Ghana Parliamentary Debates, Official Report, 26th June, 1963.
42. Ibid
43. Ghana Parliamentary Debates, Official Report, 4th July, 1963.
44. Ghana Parliamentary Debates, Official Report, 20th August, 1965.
45. Ibid
46. Ibid
47. Ibid
48. Ibid
49. Ghana Parliamentary Debates, Official Report, 27th August, 1965.
50. Ibid
51. Ibid
52. Ibid
53. Ghana Parliamentary Debates, Official Report, 30th August, 1965.
54. Ibid
55. Ibid
56. Ghana Parliamentary Debates, Official Report, 26th August, 1965.
57. Ibid

58. Ghana Parliamentary Debates, Official Report, 1st September, 1965.
59. Ibid
60. Ibid
61. Ibid
62. Ghana Parliamentary Debates, Official Report, 7th September, 1965.
63. Ibid
64. Ghana Parliamentary Debates, Official Report, 10th September, 1965.
65. Ibid
66. Ghana Parliamentary Debates, Official Report, 13th September, 1965.
67. Ibid.
68. Ghana Parliamentary Debates, Official Report, 3rd September, 1965.
69. Ibid.
70. Ibid.
71. Ibid.
72. Ghana Parliamentary Debates, Official Report, 13th September, 1965.
73. Ghana Parliamentary Debates, Official Report, 8th September, 1965.
74. Ghana Parliamentary Debates, Official Report, 13th September, 1965.
75. Ghana Parliamentary Debates, Official Report, 17th September, 1965.
76. Ibid.
77. Danquah Moses, The Birth of The Second Republic, 1969, Editorial and Publishing Services, Accra, Ghana.,p.16
78. Ibid.
79. Ibid.
80. Ghana Parliamentary Debates, Official Report, 5th March, 1970.
81. Ibid.
82. Ghana Parliamentary Debates, Official Report, 26th May, 1970.
83. Ghana Parliamentary Debates, Official Report, 10th June, 1970.

84. Ibid.
85. Ibid.
86. Ibid.
87. Ibid.
88. Ghana Parliamentary Debates, Official Report, 11th June, 1970.
89. Ibid.
90. Ibid.
91. Ghana Parliamentary Debates, Official Report, 19th May, 1970.
92. Ibid.
93. Ibid.
94. Ibid.
95. Ibid.
96. Ibid.
97. Ibid.
98. Ibid.
99. Ghana Parliamentary Debates, Official Report, 23rd June, 1970.
100. Ghana Parliamentary Debates, Official Report, 26th November, 1970.
101. Ghana Parliamentary Debates, Official Report, 4th September, 1970.
102. Ibid.
103. Ibid.
104. Danso-Boafo Kwaku, A Political Biography of Kofi Abrefa Busia, Ghana Universities Press,1996, Accra, p.153
105. Ibid.
106. Ghana Parliamentary Debates, Official Report, 28th May, 1981.
107. Ibid.
108. Ghana Parliamentary Debates, Official Report, 4th June, 1981.
109. Ibid.
110. Ghana Parliamentary Debates, Official Report, 10th June, 1981.
111. Ibid.
112. Ghana Parliamentary Debates, Official Report, 11th June, 1981.
113. Ibid.

114. Ghana Parliamentary Debates, Official Report, 12th June, 1970.
115. Ibid.

Chapter Three

WOMEN IN MILITARY REGIMES (1966 – 1992)

THE NATIONAL LIBERATION COUNCIL: Military regimes were unknown in Ghana until the 24th of February, 1966 when a group of soldiers toppled President Nkrumah and his Convention Peoples' Party government. The main reason for the coup (and the use of the word 'main' is deemed appropriate here because that is what has gained orthodoxy) was Nkrumah's overbearing leadership coupled with his establishment of a dictatorship that was feared by the people. The formation of a new government by name the National Liberation Council was announced. Lt. Gen. Joseph A. Ankrah was the Chairman. His deputy was J.W.K. Harlley who was the Inspector General of Police at the time of the coup. Other members of the council included: Lt. Col E.K. Kotoka, B.A. Yakubu, Colonel A.K. Ocran, J.E.O. Nunoo, Major A.A. Afrifa and A.K. Deku[1].The membership was entirely soldiers and policemen. Women were conspicuously absent.

The National Liberation Council abolished parliament, threw the constitution overboard and dismissed all ministers. By so doing, it took over the complete administration of the country. The Council then decided to rule the country through the issuance of decrees. These decrees became the legal basis of the various directives that were issued. For a period of about fifteen months, no civilian was made a member of the National Liberation Council. Ministerial portfolios were shared among the members[2.]

An Executive Council was established by a decree published on June

30, 1967 to include fourteen civilian commissioners with full ministerial powers[3]. The decree stated that subject to the powers of the National Liberation Council, the Executive Council was to be charged with, "the general direction and control of the Ghana Government." [4] The full Executive Council then came up to a total of twenty-two because it came to include the full membership of the council.

The following were the civilian commissioners with their responsibilities:

1. E.N. Omaboe – Ministry of Economic Affairs, Central Bureau of Statistics

2. R.S. Amegashie – Ministry of Industries, State Enterprises Secretariat

3. Victor Owusu – (Attorney-General), Ministry of Justice, Registrar – General's Department.

4. K.G. Bonsu- Ministry of Information

5. F. Ribeiro-Ayeh – Ministry of Trade.

6. J.V.L. Phillips – Ministry of Lands and Natural Resources

7. Modjaben Dowuona – Ministry of Education.

8. J. Ofori Torto – Ministry of Agriculture and Forestry.

9. Dr. E. Akwei – Ministry of Health.

10. Dr. Alex A.Y. Kyerematen – Ministry of Local Government.

11. P. D. Anin – Ministry of Communications.

12. Issifu Ali – Ministry of Works and Housing.

13. S.T. Nettey – Ministry of Labour and Social Welfare.

14. Ibrahim Mahama – Secretariats and Departments under the National Liberation Council[5]. The commissioners were sworn in at the castle by Chief Justice Edward Akuffo Addo on July 2nd 1967. [6]

A History of Women in Politics in Ghana 1957-1992

The Executive Council became the highest decision-making body of the nation. It could be compared in many respects to the Executive arm of a democratic government and it functioned as the cabinet of the nation.

In furtherance of its vision to bring about economic progress and political stability, a National Advisory Committee was formed on July 7th, 1967, a week after the formation of the Executive Council[7]. The National Advisory Committee of the National Liberation Council was made up of the following people:

1. Dr. K.A. Busia – Chairman
2. Nene Azzu Mate Kole – Vice Chairman
3. Albert Adomako – Member
4. Dr. Kportufe Agama – Member
5. Dr. E. Akwei – Member
6. Issifu Ali – Member
7. R.S. Amegashie – Member
8. Patrick D. Anin – Member
9. S.G. Antor – Member
10. M.K. Apaloo – Member
11. Ribeiro Ayeh – Member
12. Akua Asabea Ayisi – Member
13. Rev. C.G. Baeta – Member
14. B.A. Bentum – Member
15. Dr. E.V.C. de Graft Johnson – Member
16. S.D. Dombo – Member

17. Modjaben Dowuona – Member

18. M.C. Hagan – Member

19. Dr. K. G. Konuah – Member

20. Dr. A.A.Y. Kyerematen – Member

21. Ayishetu Ibrahim – Member

22. Ibrahim Mahama – Member

23. S.T. Nettey – Member

24. Prof. L.H. Ofosu-Appiah – Member

25. E.N. Omaboe – Member

26. K. G. Osei-Bonsu – Member

27. Victor Owusu – Member

28. J.V.L. Phillips – Member

29. Ruby Quartey –Papafio – Member

30. J. Ofori Torto – Member

31. Anthony Woode – Member.[8]

The main pre-occupation of the committee was to put Ghana on the road to economic progress and political stability.[9] This committee was a further step in the decision of the National Liberation Council to involve more civilians in the hitherto non-civilian government. This could be interpreted as a gradual shift from military rule to the civilian rule that was being clamoured for.

One remarkable thing about the National Advisory Committee was that for the first time, women were brought into the mainstream political activities of the council. Ayishetu Ibrahim, Akua Asabea Ayisi and Ruby Quartey-Papafio as has already been mentioned were the women who were appointed to the committee.

The National Advisory Committee existed for a year and was dissolved. Its chairman and some of its members served in the political committee of the National Liberation Council. The Political Committee acted as a team of consultants who provided advice to the council on how to return the country to civilian rule.

In 1969, the National Liberation Council conducted elections and returned the country to civilian rule having done very little to project women politically within the three and a half years that it ruled the nation.

THE NATIONAL REDEMPTION COUNCIL: The Progress Party of Dr. Kofi Abrefa Busia that took over from the National Liberation Council did not stay long in power. Twenty-eight months after assuming office a group of soldiers came and with the lofty intention of "redeeming" the country, overthrew the constitutionally elected government in the early hours of January 13, 1972.[10] The coup was reportedly bloodless and was led by Lt. Col. Ignatius Kutu Acheampong.[11]

Colonel Acheampong announced in a radio broadcast on the same day that Dr. Busia had been dismissed as Prime Minister and so was Edward Akuffo-Addo as President of the Republic.[12] The new Head of State also announced that the constitution had been withdrawn. As a result, Parliament was also dissolved. All former Ministers and Members of Parliament were required to "report to the nearest police station for their own safety".[13]

Colonel Acheampong then formed the National Redemption Council. The membership of the National Redemption Council was on January 14 announced to consist of six officers and one civilian. The only civilian was E.N. Moore, the President of the Ghana Bar Association, who was appointed Attorney-General.[14] On January 15, however, it was announced that the National Redemption Council had the following nine members: Colonel Acheampong, Air Marshal N. Ashley-Lassen (newly appointed Chief of the Defence Staff), Colonel E.A. Erskine (Army Chief of Staff), Commodore P.F. Quaye (Chief of Naval Staff), Air Marshal Charles Beausoleil (Air Force Commander), Major A.J. Selormey, Major R. M. Baah, Major K.B. Agbo and J.H. Cobbina (newly appointed Inspector General of Police) E.N. Moore lost his membership of the council but retained the post of Attorney-General.

Three officers named as National Redemption Council Members on Jan. 14, however, lost their membership. Seven local Army Commanders were appointed Commissioners of the country's regions.[15]

Further changes were made on January 29. The formation of a 13-member quasi-cabinet consisting of commissioners including only one civilian was announced. The following were the distribution of portfolios:

1. Col. I.K. Acheampong – Defence, Finance and Economic Affairs

2. Maj. General Nathan A. Aferi- Foreign Affairs

3. J.H. Cobbina – Internal Affairs

4. E.N. Moore – Justice and Attorney General

5. Maj. General Daniel Addo – Agriculture

6. Air Marshal N. Ashley-Lassen – Trade, Industry and Tourism

7. Major Asante – Labour and Social Security

8. Lt. Col. Nkegbe – Education

9. Colonel J. T. Adjetey – Health

10. General Amenu – Transport and Communication

11. Colonel Appiah – Local Government

12. Major R.M. Baah – Land distribution and Mineral Resources.[16]

On January 1, 1974 there was a cabinet reshuffle which created a 15-member cabinet. This was the second reshuffle within a year.[17] It must be stated that up to this point, no woman had been made a member of the government. Remarkably, the National Redemption Council did nothing about the absence of women in the government. This was in spite of the support that women notably the various market women's associations, had been giving to the government. It has to be mentioned that women, especially the market folk, did give a lot of support to the National Redemption Council right from the very beginning. "Thousands of people including women of the two Makola markets and employees of the Workers Brigade... staged a massive demonstration through the principal streets of Accra in support of the National Redemption Council..."[18]. Similarly, support poured in from Tema where the market women also demonstrated their support for the government. Market women in Kumasi and Sekondi-Takoradi also showed their support for the Council through meetings they held with their respective Regional Commissioners; Lt. Col. E.A. Baidoo who was the Ashanti Regional Commissioner and Col. P.K. Agyekum who was the Western Regional Commissioner[19].

The council expressed its appreciation for all these demonstrations of support but did little to translate this appreciation into appointments as commissioners or to other governmental positions. Perhaps the possible non-involvement of women in the planning and execution of the coup was the reason for this.

It was, however, the National Redemption Council regime which put into practice the United Nation's 1975 Mexico Declaration of the International Decade for Women. This was evident in the Council's establishment of the National Councilon Women and Development in 1975.[20] The National Council on Women and Development was established by NRC Decree 322.[21] The United Nations by this declaration drew the attention of member nations to the need to set up national commissions and agencies to look into the status of women and find ways and means of improving the role of women in the world community in general and the individual member countries in particular.[22] Member countries were expected to eventually, "develop action plans that would lead to the improvement of the position of women in their respective countries."[23] "The National Council on Women and Development had the major role of advising the government on all matters relating to the full integration of women in national development." [24] The National Council on Women and Development did not involve itself in the field of politics but that political empowerment of Ghanaian women was very important on its programmes was without doubt. One of its official responsibilities was clear, "To serve as the official national body for co-operating, coordinating and liaising with national and international organisations on matters relating to the status of women."[25] The activities of the Council, however, depicted it as a non-political organisation.

FROM NRC TO SMC: The name of the government was changed from National Redemption Council to Supreme Military Council. This change was not very significant because basically, the same military officers continued to be in the government and under the same leadership. Not surprisingly, very little was done to change the nearly apolitical situation of Ghanaian women.

In the course of the life of the SMC one issue that came up was that the Chairman of the Supreme Military Council, General Acheampong, was involved in some corrupt practices detrimental to the developmental efforts of the Supreme Military Council and by extension the country. This was the reason given for a coup d'etat that resulted in the launching of the second phase of the Supreme Military Council which has come to be popularly known as SMC II.[26] The SMC II was an offshoot of the Supreme Military Council which is now popularly referred to as SMC I. The most significant aspect of this change was in terms of headship. General Frederick William K. Akuffo became the Head of State in what was a bloodless palace coup. This was in July 1978.[27] There was no major change in the directive principles of state policy and the political position of women was not expected to change.

From the time the National Redemption Council overthrew the Busia administration to 1978, there was no woman in top national political activity until the appointment by the Supreme Military Council II of Gloria Nikoi, as a Commissioner in January, 1979. Mrs. Nikoi, a distinguished public servant was appointed as the commissioner for Foreign Affairs. Her appointment, "was a time of jubilation for women who were conscious of the importance of, and the need for effective political participation of women in the nation's affairs. A delegation of the Federation of Market Women's Association in Accra called at her office to congratulate her on her appointment."[28] She was a graduate of St. Andrews University in Scotland where she graduated with a Master of Arts degree in Economics and Modern History in 1952. Prior to her appointment, she had served as a Research Fellow in the then University of the Gold Coast (now University of Ghana) between 1952 and 1954. She then served as an assistant secretary at the ministries of Trade and Finance. Between 1959 and 1961, she served at the United Nations Secretariat as a Political Officer. She rose to the post of Deputy Chief of Mission at the Ghana Embassy in Washington. From 1969 to 1974 she occupied the post of Supervising Director of Economic Relations Department of the Ministry of Foreign Affairs.[29] She held other portfolios and distinguished herself in all of them. Part of a tribute paid in her honour in a contemporary newspaper is worth quoting, "The seat of Foreign Affairs Minister or Commissioner poses enormous challenges for whoever occupies it. Such challenges call for a tactful diplomacy, experience and vivid imagination. And Mrs. Gloria Amon Nikoi the first woman to be in the seat and in fact the first woman commissioner in the country has a combination of all the pre-requisites to make her a good commissioner"[30.] On her experiences, the tribute went on, "Mrs. Nikoi occupied the post of Supervising Director of Economic Relations Department of the Foreign Affairs Ministry from 1969 to 1974 until her promotion to the rank of Principal Secretary in 1970. And in 1974 she was seconded from Foreign Service and was appointed to serve as a permanent member of the newly constituted National Economic Planning Council. In 1977, when she was promoted to the rank of Senior Principal Secretary she also became the chairman of the External Debt Committee of the Ministry of Finance..."[31]. On the occasion of her swearing in Gloria Nikoi said she saw the honour done her not only as an honour to herself but an honour to the profession she belonged to.[32] She also added that she saw her appointment as a tribute to the great contribution that Ghanaian women had made to the political and social life of the country. [33]

In her duties, Gloria Nikoi worked to establish a good relationship between Ghana and other countries. At a luncheon for outgoing Canadian High Commissioner in Ghana, Robert Morrice Middleton, she praised the government of Canada, "for maintaining an effective bilateral relations between her and other Third World Countries." [34] She observed that this was the kind of relationship that should exist between the developed world and the developing countries saying, "in 1977 Canadian disbursements to Ghana in various technical and economic aid programmes were the highest amount of official development assistance from any external donor" and that "the current Canadian International Development Agency allocation for Ghana would make Ghana the second largest recipient of Canadian external assistance in

Africa."³⁵ This, she said, underscored the closeness of the relationship between the two countries.³⁶ Gloria Nikoi did a lot of work in terms of meeting envoys, signing bilateral agreements and leading delegations to other countries.

THE ARMED FORCES REVOLUTIONARY COUNCIL: Six months after the appointment of Gloria Nikoi and with a few days to presidential and parliamentary elections, the government of the Supreme Military Council was overthrown. The new government was the Armed Forces Revolutionary Council led by an Air Force Officer, Flt. Lt. Jerry John Rawlings.

The Armed Forces Revolutionary Council said it had no intention of staying in power for long. It was made up of fifteen young men who were junior officers and other ranks in the Ghana Armed Forces. Apart from Jerry Rawlings, the following belonged to the Council: Boakye-Djan, Baah-Acheamfour, Mensah Poku, Alex Adjei, Henry Akpaloo, Ansah Atiemo, Sarkodee Addo, Peter Tasiri, Newton Katsiko, Sheikh Tetteh, Mensah Gbedema, Harry Obeng, Owusu Addae, Owusu Boateng and Kwesi Adu.³⁷ According to Jerry Rawlings, the council's intention of seizing power was to undertake a process of "house cleaning". ³⁸ One would remember that seven years prior to the advent of the council, Ghana had been ruled almost entirely by military officers. The view of some of the junior officers and the non-officer core of the army was that many of the senior officers of the army who were ruling the country had denigrated the image of the army.³⁹ The extent to which this had been done was, in their opinion, very high. If nothing was done to, as it were, clean the house of the army, a future civilian administration in particular and the civilian population in general would not accord the army their due respect and pride of place. The impending elections and the scheduled timetable for hand-over, notwithstanding, a coup must take place and the house of the military must be cleaned. This was in the view of the coup makers the rationale behind the coup⁴⁰. Some officers were targeted to be part of the "refuse" of the "house" and consequently "swept". The result was the killing of many high ranking officers. Notable among them were: General I.K. Acheampong, General F.W.K. Akuffo, Rear Admiral Joy Amedume.

The Armed Forces Revolutionary Council met the presidential candidates of the various parties and assured them that the June 18th date would not be changed. "After some discussions it was agreed that the parliamentary and presidential elections would proceed as arranged on 18th June, but that the handing over would be postponed for three months to 1st October to allow the AFRC to complete its task".[42]

As stated earlier, the Council had no intention of staying in power for long. As a result, they did not concern themselves very much with the business of forming and running a government in the proper sense of the word. General Joshua Hamidu had been a member of the overthrown Supreme Military Council. He was not killed with his colleagues because Jerry Rawlings and his men thought him to be a disciplined and honest man.[43] Seeing himself inexperienced in the art of government and desiring to exert some direct control over the army, Jerry Rawlings appointed Joshua Hamidu to head a defacto government.[44] Kevin Shillington's account of the circumstances surrounding the appointment of General Hamidu is worth quoting "... Hamidu was anxious to salvage some kind of role for the senior officer corps and from his point of view, it was their duty to relieve Flight Lieutenant Rawlings of as much responsibility as possible. At the same time Hamidu felt that in the long-term interest of the military hierarchy, the senior officer corps should divert itself of the sort of total control of government which it had exercised in Acheampong's time. Civilians should be more fully involved in the top levels of government. The economist Dr. J.L.S. Abbey, Commissioner for Finance in the Akuffo government, was brought in on these discussions and he recommended that, for the sake of administrative stability, the civilians of the previous government should be left in place at the head of the various ministries. This, he argued, would leave Rawlings and the AFRC free to decide on policy directives and to control the precarious military situation. Rawlings acted on this advice and appointed General Hamidu as Liaison Officer between the ministries and the AFRC – in effect a sort of Prime Minister – a position which Hamidu exploited to the full. Seeing himself as an important balancing factor in the uncertain times ahead, Hamidu moved into the castle, the official seat of government, while Rawlings was based in Burma Camp throughout the period of AFRC rule."[45]

Jerry Rawlings handed over to President Hilla Limann on 24th September 1979 and the Third Republic of Ghana was thus formally inaugurated in Parliament House in Accra. Jerry Rawlings made a brief but significant speech shortly before the handing over. Part of that speech read thus: "never before have the eyes of so many been focused on so few, Mr. President. The few are you, the illustrious members of our new civilian administration. The many are those in the factories and on the farms, in the dormitories and junior quarters who will be watching you, with eagles' eyes to see whether the change they are hoping for will actually materialize in their lifetime... we know you will deliver the goals. That is why we have turned a deaf ear to those who have entreated us to stay on a little longer, because our job is not complete. We have every confidence that we shall never regret our decision to go back to barracks." [46]

President Limann stayed in power for twenty-seven months. What happened to the political position of women during his tenure as President is subject matter for another chapter of this text.

THE PROVISIONAL NATIONAL DEFENCE COUNCIL: On December 31, 1981, the government of Dr. Limann was overthrown by his predecessor, Jerry Rawlings. Not only was Dr. Limann overthrown but the entire political machinery of the Republic including the Parliament was also suspended. Political parties were proscribed and all government appointees were sacked.[47]

Rawlings in his maiden broadcast to the nation said among others, "... this is not a coup. I ask for nothing less than a revolution – something that will transform the social and economic order of this country[48] "Fellow citizens, it is now left to you to decide how this country is going to go from today. We are asking for nothing more than popular democracy. We are asking for nothing more than the power to organize this country in such a way that nothing will be done from the castle without the consent and authority of the people. In other words, the people, the farmers, the police, the soldiers, the workers-you, the guardians- rich or poor, should be a part of the decision-making process of this country." [49]

Right from the onset, Rawlings set himself the task of practicalising his revolutionary concept in what was to become the longest running military regime in the history of the country. What was presented as the rationale for seizing power was the establishment of an entirely new and expectedly effective system of what Rawlings called "popular democracy". [50] The phrases "people's participatory democracy" and "participation in the decision-making process" were to become the catch-phrases of the revolution which set itself the task of reshaping Ghanaian society.

Rawlings announced the formation of a government known as the Provisional National Defence Council. This was the result of a decree published on January 11th, 1982.[51] The decree formally set out structurally and functionally what the Provisional National Defence Council was all about. "The council assumed all the executive powers of government. Rawlings was chairman and the other members were Brigadier Nunoo-Mensah, the Chief of Defence Staff, Rev. Dr. Vincent Kwabina Damuah, a Catholic Priest with a strong record of service among the poor; Warrant Officer Joseph Adjei Buadi; Co-ordinator of the Armed Forces' Defence Committees; Sergeant Alolga Akata-Pore, an active member of the left-wing Movement on National Affairs (MONAS) and a recent student of economics at the University of Cape Coast; Joachim Amartey Kwei, former Secretary-General of the GIHOC Workers' Union and the only civilian to have been actively involved in the coup; and Chris Bukari Atim, Secretary of the June Fourth Movement. The decree allowed for the appointment of further members to the council, up to a maximum of eleven. "[51]

To have massive support for the new revolution, the Provisional National Defence Council leader, Chairman Rawlings, as he became popularly known, decided to mobilize as many people as possible. In the workplaces, Workers Defence Committees were formed with the intention of giving workers an extraordinary say in what went on at the workplaces. In some cases, they nearly took over the management of their workplaces and even recommended the dismissal of colleague workers that they perceived to be non-performing. In communities, Peoples' Defence Committees were formed with the aim of giving ordinary Ghanaians a say in the management of their communities.[53]

More relevant to this work is the mobilization of women as part of the new revolution. It must be mentioned that the Provisional National Defence Council came at a time when many of the customs and traditions that had made women to play second fiddle in the Ghanaian society were still existent. To a large extent, Ghanaian women were still not emancipated. Rawlings, in a bid to ensure the success of the revolution that he had launched, urged women to compete keenly with men in all aspects of national life. Invariably, he saw a keen participation of women as reflective of the success of the revolution. To him, his coming had provided an opportunity for Ghanaian women not to, "feel neglected, inferior and relegated to the background."[54] To symbolize the emancipation of Ghanaian women, he presented a loaded rifle to a woman at a rally of workers, artisans and peasants at Bolgatanga and he called on women to accept the big challenge.[55] In advising them to accept the challenge, he paid tribute to Princess Amina of Nigeria and Nana Yaa Asantewaa of Edweso in Ashanti and called on Ghanaian women to draw an inspiration from these two great symbols of feminine courage and determination.[56]

Three weeks after seizing power, he made a number of appointments of people to head some ministries.

These were:

Appiah Korang	-	Fuel and Power
K.B. Asante	-	Trade
J.A. Kufour	-	Local Government
Ama Ata Aidoo	-	Education
Kwaku Ankomah	-	Rural Development and Co-operatives
Johnny Hansen	-	Internal Affairs
Asiedu Yirenkyi	-	Culture and Tourism
Zaya Yebo	-	Youth and Sports
Dr. Obed Asamoah	-	Foreign Affairs
Ato Austin	-	Information
Iddrisu Mahama	-	Transport and Communication
Dr. Kaku Kyiamah	-	Industry, Science and Technology

Prof. Mawuse Dake	-	Works and Housing
G.E.K. Aikins	-	Justice and Attorney General
Prof. Bortei-Doku	-	Agriculture
Saara Mensah	-	Brong Ahafo Region
Atukwei Okai	-	Greater Accra Region.[57]

Another set of appointment of ministerial heads, this time including some deputies, were as follows:

Dr. Don Arthur	-	Ministry of Roads and Highways
Kofi Acquaah Harrison	-	Central Region
Gertrude Zakaria	-	Deputy, Local Government
Kwesi Kammassa	-	Deputy, Volta Region
Adam Kaleem	-	Deputy, Agriculture[58]

These heads and deputies came to be known as secretaries. By their appointments they became the political heads of the various ministries and acted as liaison between the council and the ministries. Two women were appointed. These were, as indicated above, Ama Ata Aidoo and Gertrude Zakaria.

As secretary for the very turbulent ministry of Education, Ama Ata Aidoo had to put up a tough posture in her duties. She spoke vehemently against violent student agitations which were erroneously considered to be a part of the new revolution. Student agitations in the form of violent demonstrations resulting in the destruction of properties had taken place in schools in Anloga, Dzodze, Bechem, Techiman, Abetifi, Tamale, Navrongo and Sogakope. These prompted her to make a live radio and television broadcast to the nation.[59]

Ama Ata Aidoo's agitations were crucial in the establishment of what was later to be known as the Junior Secondary Schools and the Senior Secondary Schools. At a biennial national delegates conference of the Ghana National Association of Teachers in Kumasi, she described the then educational system as, "elitist which is geared towards the production of too many white-collar personnel". [60] She said it was a mark of irresponsibility for a government to observe this and, "sit idly for such a despicable thing to go on un-checked". [61] Invariably she was advocating a re-structuring of the educational system which resulted in the phasing out of the Middle School, Ordinary Level and Advanced Level systems. Ama Ata Aidoo was very much at the forefront of the call for increased morality, sense of responsibility and a general increase in patriotism in the ordinary Ghanaian. The various regimes prior to the advent of the Provisional National Defence Council had generally been accused as lacking these. In her view, the way and manner parents treated their children whilst they were young and still at home was key to the solution of the numerous problems that confronted the country. At a rally organized by the Accra District branch of Christian Mothers Association in Accra, she blamed educated Ghanaians for having contributed immensely to bring down the nation. She, therefore, called on the Mothers, "to bring up their children in such a way that their minds would be brought back to the woes of the country to enable them to rebuild it."[62] She told the gathering, "We are the only people who can help because we are responsible for bringing up the children in the home". In her view, governments that had failed the nation had failed the nation because people who made up the government were not properly brought up in their homes.[63]

At the inauguration of the 31st December Women's Movement, the Deputy Secretary for Local Government who was also a member of the Movement, Gertrude Zakaria called on the government to do something about the economic deterioration of Ghanaian women when she requested the release of the Makola market in Accra to Ghanaian women through the movement[64] and said since women accepted December 31 as a new era, they must ensure that the movement had come to stay to help make the country a better place to live in. [65] Gertrude Zakaria was not merely an ordinary official of the government but one that within the bigger picture of national development, was pushing an agenda for the betterment of the economic well-being of Ghanaian women. She did this very often. Though the December 31st Women's Movement sought to appear as a non-governmental and non-political organisation, the activities of Gertrude Zakaria and others were to portray it, in the eyes of many Ghanaians, not merely as political but as an integral arm of the revolution.

As part of activities marking a World Food Day celebration in Accra, Gertrude Zakaria admonished Ghanaians to form co-operatives since that was a way of ensuring efficient and maximum utilization of available resources to ensure higher productivity.[66] She called on women to use the occasion to assess themselves and take a re-look at the factors that militate against their efforts at food sufficiency and find means of combating them.[67]

The first half of 1982 (the first year of the December 31st revolution) saw no woman as a member of the Provisional National Defence Council. In August of that same year, three key members of government resigned. These were Rev. Dr. Vincent Kwabena Damuah and Joachim Amartey Kwei who were both members of the Provisional National Defence Council and John Agyekum Kufour who was the Secretary responsible for Local Government.[68]

To beef up the government, fresh appointments were made. Aanaa Enin who was Marketing Manager of the State Fishing Corporation and Ebo Tawiah who was the Chairman of the Interim Management Committee of the Maritime and Dockworkers Union were appointed as Provisional National Defence Council members to replace Rev. Damuah and Amartey Kwei.[69]

Before being appointed a member of the Council, Aanaa Enin had "been active in working with other women towards building up a national women's organisation" [70] through her activities as a leading member of the Federation of Ghanaian Women Associations. By her appointment, she became privy to decisions taken at the executive level of government. Mention has to be made of the fact that functionally, the council was the cabinet of the nation under the PNDC. Executive decisions emanated from the Council and the council members went with the designation "PNDC Member." PNDC Members were involved in deliberations that affected all aspects of government and were involved in policy formulation and monitoring. They were also the spokespersons and defenders of the ideologies of the revolution. Such was the magnitude of the task Aanaa Enin saw herself being charged with.

She played a key role in the Provisional National Defence Council and was instrumental in a lot of successes and goodwill that the government enjoyed in the early years of its rule. Being a woman, she sought to use her position in the council to demonstrate that women had a part to play in the revolution for she believed that "no revolution can succeed without the active participation of women." [71] She, therefore, called on women to unite and decried the fact that women's groups had been based on religious, social and professional inclinations with very narrow scopes of activity. She was of the view that women were too fragmented in organisation to be meaningful.[72] "We have to come together first and foremost as women participating in the on-going revolutionary process. The professional, religious and social labels should take second place. The unity of women as she saw it was not merely to unite women to make them stronger but also to provide the mass support that the government needed in the formative years of its appearance on the political scene. This was crucial for the government if one considers the fact that the government overthrew a popularly elected government.

She very often defended the policies of the Provisional National Defence Council. As a member of the council and a partaker in its decisions one would say that she could not have acted otherwise but again this is a role that was very crucial to the survival of the government. This is so especially if one looks at the era of the PNDC against the backdrop that the country had been the playing field of varied political ideologies all of which had been perceived to have done very little about the socio-economic circumstances of Ghanaians. The doubt expressed, therefore, was whether this new revolution being espoused would be different from the regimes that preceded it. Speaking at a ceremony at the Soviet Cultural Centre at Osu in Accra, she stressed that the aim of the Provisional National Defence Council was, "to transform the society from exploitation and dictatorship to an egalitarian and a genuine democratic society in which everybody would have a stake in the political direction of the country."[74] She, therefore, appealed for the support of "friendly countries to help push forward the aims and objectives of the December 31st Revolution." [75]

Aanaa Enin took up the call for emancipation and democratisation; this time at the larger African continental level. Apartheid was being practised in South Africa at the time the Provisional National Defence Council came into power. There were calls across the world to end this system of government since it was seen generally not only to be obsolete but inhumane as well. At a meeting with Ivorian Ambassador political appointment, he was espousing why I should. I asked for time to think about it. At home I heard over the radio that I had been made a member of the PNDC." [80]

Although Susanna Al-Hassan spent a relatively short time as PNDC member, she nevertheless did make a more than ordinary impact. At the First All African Wood Fair in Accra, she called on timber operators "to protect Ghana's canopy of forests by avoiding...indiscriminate felling of trees." She also charged them "to encourage the use of the lesser known species to help popularize them, thereby shifting the... dependence on the known species". She urged the foreign exhibitors who had come to the exhibition to find areas of co-operation and partnership to boost the country's export trade. [81]

The socialist inclinations which were a part of the Nkrumah government in the early years of the attainment of independence were seen to be in Susanna Al-Hassan when she joined the PNDC. Not only was she seen clamouring indirectly for a socialist approach to the nation's problems locally but was also to push for a deepening of relationships with socialist-inclined countries. At a meeting with V.M. Semenov, Russian Ambassador to Ghana, she concerned herself with "co-operation in the fields of education, industry, health and the effective mobilization of Ghanaian women."[82] At the same time, she was conscious of the unnecessary tension she might create between Ghana and countries of the capitalist world. In another discussion, this time with Radivoje Petkovic, Yugoslavian Ambassador, she called on the Non-Aligned Movement to become more dynamic.[83] The Non-Aligned Movement was an organisation of countries that within the era of the Cold War were clear that they were neither on the side of the communist East nor capitalist West. These countries were mostly developing countries in Africa and Asia. President Tito of Yugoslavia and President Nkrumah of Ghana were some of the founding fathers of the Movement. Ghana and Yugoslavia played an active role in the affairs of the Movement.

The Kumasi Shoe Factory and the Asutsuare Sugar Factory which operated in Ghana briefly before collapsing were all sponsored by the government of Czechoslovakia. The resuscitation of these projects was the subject for discussion when Ambassador Ladislov Sobr of the Republic of Czechoslovakia met Susanna Al-Hassan for bilateral discussions.[86] She "commended the government and the people of Czechoslovakia for their continued support for Africa in the fight against apartheid and the liberation struggle."[87] As has already been mentioned, this era coincided with the apartheid era of South Africa. At this time, the fight against apartheid had been intensified and all resources were being marshalled against the racist government of South Africa.

Susanna Al-Hassan also played host to United States Ambassador to Ghana, Robert Fritts. This was prior to a donors' conference slated for Paris. Ambassador Fritts told her the United States and other donor countries as well as the World Bank were working out the possibilities of assisting Ghana to overcome her storage problem in the post-harvest period.[84] She on her part "expressed warm sentiments about the healthy relations between Ghana and the United States and hoped the situation will continue for the common good of the two countries."[85] Eighteen months after accepting to work with the PNDC, Susanna Al-Hassan asked to be relieved of her duties on grounds of ill-health. Apparently, a generally hectic schedule as Council member was taking a toll on her health.

Another woman who played a leading role in the political activities of the council was Joyce Aryee. She was not a member for the council per se. She was one of the Secretaries that were appointed to head ministries. She began with her acceptance to head the Ministry of Information in 1983.[89] She functioned in that capacity as the mouthpiece of the government. At a meeting with a delegation from the United Nations Educational Scientific and Cultural Organisation, she said the government was doing its best in the face of difficulties in keeping pace with ever-advancing technology in the mass media.[90] Bureaucratically, she was the liaison between the government and the media as far as dissemination of official government information was concerned. In a discussion with the Australian High Commissioner to Ghana, she affirmed that the activities of the government in the form of the Economic Recovery Programme were intended to weaken the nation's over-dependence on other countries for essential commodities. This way, she said, the sovereignty of the country would be strengthened. She called for assistance not only in material terms but also in the form of better understanding and goodwill.[91] About the achievements of the government, she told the High Commissioner, "our achievements are modest, at least we know we have taken the right path and...that friends will appreciate the bold stand we have taken to assist us move forward."[92]

A reshuffle in portfolios in 1984 saw Joyce Aryee heading the Ministry of Education. Her stay there was eventful: it marked two very important developments. One was the introduction of a new school uniform that was to be used in basic schools all over the country. This was irrespective of whether the school was a mission school, owned by a local authority or privately owned. Objections were raised to this directive. This, notwithstanding, the measure was adopted and schools changed to the new uniform. The introduction of educational reforms was another landmark in the life of Joyce Aryee as the head of the education ministry. This reform saw the phasing out of the Middle School, Ordinary Level and Advanced Level system and certificates. In their place came the Junior Secondary and the Senior Secondary School system with new Certificates.[93]

She also was involved in energizing the youth. She was a young person herself when she came into office. After a peace march by elementary school children in Accra, she spoke to them urging them to take responsibility since the future belonged to them. According to her, the time was up "for the youth and the older people to sit together and think out a future for this country and the world at large."[94] In another address to the All African Kindness Club, she again stressed on peace saying, "the world's greatest concern... was for peace in order to develop." [95]

She, therefore, called for a "type of education which will make the educated person want to live with others, but not to be above others." 96 This was because "it was only the education of the heart, making people feel for others, which will bring peace and ensure that each man is his brother's keeper." [97] She was influenced in her office by her religious principles. She was a staunch Christian woman. Not only that, she was an active member of the Young Women's Christian Association.

This influenced her in her campaign against war and violence and her advocacy for increased human rights.[98]

Vida Yeboah, a former headmistress of Mfantseman Girls Secondary School at Saltpond who had been the Deputy Director in charge of the National Service Scheme was appointed in 1985 to the position of Deputy Secretary of Education alongside Walter K. Blege.[99] Vida Yeboah placed her vast experience as a long-serving teacher at the disposal of the government. The administrative work of the ministry, particularly at the basic level, came directly under her. She was instrumental in the upgrading of some junior secondary schools, especially in the rural areas, into secondary schools. This was intended to procure placements for the about 53,000 pupils that were expected to form the first batch of graduates of the Junior Secondary School system.[100] Her experience as a person with a long career in teaching101 came in handy. She was competent and was relied upon in the work of setting out "the content and structure of secondary education"[102] in Ghana. A lot of her practical ideas came to be factored in the new curriculum that was adopted for use at the Senior Secondary School Level.

The education sector in the era of the Provisional National Defence Council indeed was the major beneficiary of the immense experience of great Ghanaian women. Ama Ata Aidoo, Joyce Aryee, and Vida Yeboah were some of these women. Another woman whose contribution to education cannot be downplayed was Esi Sutherland Addy. Her appointment as Deputy Secretary in the Ministry of education provided her with the opportunity to make a contribution which can be said to be extraordinary.

Prior to her appointment in September 1986, which came with a reshuffling of portfolios, she had been the Deputy Secretary for Culture and Tourism which position she had taken in March of that same year.[103] Though she did hold it for a brief spell of time, her contribution in that position was great. This was a very comfortable position since she was a specialist in African Oral Literature and Folklore and had indeed read for her master's degree in that field.[104] Her contribution in the education ministry is what Esi Sutherland Addy is most remembered for.

The Ministry of Education was without doubt the foundation for policy making in respect of training the manpower needs of the country.

The raw material in this manpower training was the youth. One can, therefore, appreciate Esi Sutherland Addy's advocacy against drug abuse among the youth. Not only was she interested in fighting the menace as she saw it in the youth but also believed that parents had to be roped in "to make the youth aware that the aspirations of the nation are different from that of the developed world and thus they should not emulate the practices of the developed world."[105] She also urged societies, church groups and parents to come together to promote "meaningful child training programmes to prevent the youth from indulging in drug abuse and other vices." [106] The seriousness of drug abuse in Ghana in the 1980s which warranted her concern can be viewed against the background of a society that was becoming increasingly engulfed in the habit. Dr. J.B. Asare of the Accra Psychiatric Hospital was on a crusade in second cycle schools against the menace.

One can, therefore, appreciate Dr. Mary Grant's concern when as Deputy Secretary for Health, she was called upon to address a World Health Organisation "consultative meeting on assessment of standard care for drug abuse." [107] She expressed the Ghana government's determination to fight the menace of drug abuse to ensure the growth of the economy and the survival of the youth." She viewed the issue seriously since the effect on the nation was not only in terms of its destruction of the youth but the fact that "money has to be found to fight it." [108] The issue indeed needed addressing if one looked at the fact that Ghana was increasingly becoming a strategic location in terms of transit for drug barons from across the world.

The need to manage the population of Ghana to prevent a situation of inadequate resources coming under pressure from a highly populated country was one of the issues at play in the 1980s. The 1984 population census had revealed the need to reduce the rate of childbirth in order to ensure that population increased at an optimum level. This was a way of improving the quality of life of Ghanaians. As Deputy Secretary for Health, Dr. Mary Grant was actively involved in family life management and was a crucial role player in the fight to change the misconceptions and erroneous impressions that majority of Ghanaians had about population and family life issues.[109] She called for a lot of education to be done and was ready to help couples "understand and realize that such programmes are not directed merely at the physical reduction or to discourage childbirth but to help improve the quality of life for both the mothers and their children." [110] After the expulsion of Aanaa Enin from the PNDC as a Council Member, Dr. Mary Grant was made a Council Member. She continued to be a member of the council and continued to work for the government till the ushering in of the Fourth Republican constitutional rule. Her duties included receiving envoys for and on behalf of the government and canvassing for support for the government, especially from Ghanaian women.[111]

In assessing the contribution of Ghanaian women to the Provisional National Defence Council regime, mention also has to be made of Francisca Issaka and Theresa Owusu who as Deputy Secretaries for Local Government and Fuel and Power respectively did contribute their quota to the regime and through it the nation. Francisca Issaka was involved in efforts to sustain the district assembly concept and make it fruitful. Seeing it as the bulwark against underdevelopment, poverty and depravity, she was of the view that district assemblies must "submit their budgetary proposals to government on time for approval." [112] This, in her view, would prevent unnecessary delays and instead, speed up the rate of development of the country.

Apart from her regular schedule at the Ministry of Fuel and Power, Theresa Owusu engaged herself in activities to promote efforts at helping destitutes in the Ghanaian society. At a ceremony to mark the fifteenth anniversary of the SOS Children's Association of Ghana, she called on the Ghanaian society to see the need to care and sustain abandoned children since these were noble and commendable objectives which should even win the understanding and support of all well-meaning people in the world. [113] In her view, efforts must continually be made jointly by the government and Ghanaians generally "to provide appropriate care and humanitarian services for the orphaned, destitute and abandoned children." [114]

Beside women who held positions in the council and positions of ministerial ranking in the era under discussion, there were numerous other women who held appointive positions at the district assembly level. President Nkrumah's pioneering appointment of Ramatu Baba as the first female District Commissioner (for Yendi) in the 1960s[115] had launched a phenomenon that was only to be equalled under the Provisional National Defence Council regime which appointed several women as District secretaries (the equivalent of district commissioners which is also equivalent to district chief executives). Notable among them included Grace Amma Serwa Hanson (Amansie West) [116], Sarah Kuntu-Atta (Mfantseman), [117] Georgina Bus-Kwofie (Ahanta West) [118], Christine Churcher (Cape Coast) [119] and the phenomenal Rose Oteng (Asante-Akim North) during whose tenure the Asante-Akim North District Assembly set up the Asante-Akim North Development Company Limited.[120] This was meant to be the commercial wing of the district administration. The intention was to use this limited liability company to raise revenue to create employment and at the same time provide money to develop the district.[121]

In appreciating the role Aanna Enin, Efua Sutherland, Gertrude Zakaria, Ama Ata Aidoo, Joyce Aryee and all the host of the many other women played in the Provisional National Defence Council era, one has to look at issues from two perspectives. One is from the perspective of their contribution in respect of their advocacy roles and the crusades they assigned themselves to and its overall impact or intended impact on the society. The other is the contributions they made to ensure the survival of the Provisional National Defence Council government by acting as its eloquent spokespersons and defenders of its policies. Each of these women was outstanding in her own right prior to accepting the appointment. Ama Ata Aidoo, for instance, was an accomplished author and university lecturer, Joyce Aryee was a Public Relations Officer with Ghana Standards Board[122] whilst Esi Sutherland Addy was a university lecturer.[123]

It is worth mentioning, therefore, that their appointments were not acts of tokenism. Rather, they were a recognition of women's capabilities and capacity for service within the context of a society that was intensely patriarchal and was heavily influenced by cultural practices and belief systems that were to some extent inimical to the fairer sex.

All governments that were overthrown in this country were overthrown by a "Council" military government of some sort. The National Liberation Council overthrew the Convention People's Party government. The former handed over to the Progress Party which was also overthrown by the National Redemption Council which "council" within the course of time changed into another council. This time, it was the Supreme Military Council. The Supreme Military Council was overthrown by the Armed Forces Revolutionary Council. It handed over to the Peoples National Party. The leader of the Armed Forces Revolutionary Council and some other soldiers then came again and overthrew the government that their leader, Rawlings, handed over to. The new council that was formed this time was called the Provisional National Defence Council. What is very important is not the fact that all the military governments had the label 'councils' but the fact that over a long period of time, despite the lofty ideals espoused, these councils did very little to improve the status of women politically. The National Liberation Council did little to liberate women and rather drew back the efforts began by Nkrumah. The fate of the women in parliament in 1972 was also seriously affected by the National Redemption Council which also did not redeem the political image of women and rather kept them in the background till 1979 when its offspring, the Supreme Military Council, appointed Gloria Nikoi to head the Foreign Affairs Ministry. This was then followed by the rather shortlived government of the Armed Forces Revolutionary Council.

Again, very little was seen. The Provisional National Defence Council was a brighter spot in a dark environment. This council, which of course was the last of them, projected women politically. This was made possible by the very character of the government which sought to create a political system with a solid base through the mobilization of the support of the masses. This was done concurrently through the Peoples Defence Committees, the Workers Defence Committees, the Committee for the Defence of the Revolution and the multi-facial 31st December Women's Movement.

ENDNOTES

1. Danquah Moses, The Birth of the Second Republic, 1969, Editorial and Publishing Services, Accra, Ghana, P.16. Also, Adu Boahen, Ghana: Evolution and Change In The Nineteenth And Twentieth Centuries, Sankofa Educational Publishers Ltd., 2000, Accra. pp.225-226.
2. Africa Dairy: Weekly Record of Events in Africa, Vol. II, 1967, p. 3501
3. ibid
4. ibid
5. ibid
6. ibid
7. Ghana Gazette, 28th July, 1967 p. 485
8. Ibid
9. Ibid
10. Keesings Contemporary Archives (1971 – 1972), Vol. XVIII, Keesing's Publication Ltd., London, Keynsham BS18 2BD, Bristol, pp.25115 - 25116
11. Ibid
12. Ibid
13. Ibid
14. Ibid
15. Ibid
16. Ibid
17. Keesings Contemporary Archives (1974) Vol. XX, Keesing's Publications Ltd, Longman Group Ltd, London, p.26314
18. Daily Graphic, Friday 4th February, 1972.
19. Daily Graphic, Tuesday 25th January, 1972.
20. Brown, C.K. Women in Local Government in Ghana: A case study of Central Region, Friedrich Ebert Foundation, Accra, 1996, page 12-13.
21. Ibid
22. Ibid
23. Ibid
24. Lartey, Theresa Lartehey, "Women in Ghanaian Politics 1951 – 1990". An undergraduate dissertation presented to the Department of History, University of Ghana, Legon, June, 1991. pp 3-5.

25. Brown, C.K., Op.Cit. p.13.
26. Shillington, Kevin, Ghana and the Rawlings Factor, 1992, Macmillan Press Ltd., London. P.38.
27. Ibid
28. Lartey, Theresa Larteley, Op.Cit. p.16.
29. Daily Graphic, January 8th, 1979. p.5.
30. Ibid
31. Ibid
32. Daily Graphic, January 6th, 1979, p.1.
33. Ibid
34. Daily Graphic, January 5th 1979 pp.8 &9.
35. Ibid
36. Ibid
37. Interview with Kwaku Baako Jnr. Editor, Crusading Guide. Information given here was corroborated on phone by Capt (Ltd) Boakye Gyan a member of the Armed Forces Revolutionary Council.
38. Shillington, Kevin Op.Cit. p.46.
39. Ibid
40. Ibid
41. Interview with Kwaku Baako Jnr. Op.Cit.
42. Shillington, Kevin, Op.Cit. p.49.
43. Ibid
44. Ibid
45. Ibid
46. Ibid
47. Ibid
48. Ibid
49. Ibid
50. Ibid
51. Ibid
52. Ibid
53. Ibid. Later the Workers Defence Committees and the Peoples' Defence Committees were merged and cane under a new name, the Committee for the Defence of the Revolution; CDR as they popularly came to be called.
54. Daily Graphic, Thursday March 18th, 1982, pp 4-5.
55. Ibid
56. Ibid
57. Daily Graphic, Friday January 22nd, 1982, p.1.
58. Daily Graphic, Tuesday February 2nd, 1982, pp. 4-5.

59. Daily Graphic, Tuesday February 12th, 1982, p.1.
60. Daily Graphic, Monday August 30th, 1982, p.1.
61. Ibid
62. Daily Graphic, Monday March 29th, 1982, p.5.
63. Ibid
64. Daily Graphic, Monday May 17th, 1982, p.1.
65. Ibid
66. Daily Graphic, Tuesday October 16th, 1984, p.1.
67. Ibid
68. Daily Graphic, Thursday August 19th, 1982, p.1.
69. Ibid
70. Ibid
71. Daily Graphic, Monday August 30, 1982, p.5.
72. Daily Graphic, Tuesday September 7, 1982, p.1.
73. Ibid
74. Daily Graphic, Monday October 11th, 1982, p.1.
75. Ibid
76. Daily Graphic, Friday October 29th, 1982, p.1.
77. Ibid
78. Ibid
79. Daily Graphic, Wednesday October 25th, 1989, p.1.
80. Vieta, Kojo Flag bearers of Ghana, ENA Publications, 2000, Accra, p125
81. Daily Graphic, Monday April 8th, 1985, p.1.
82. Daily Graphic, Wednesday November 7th, 1984, p.9
83. Ibid
84. Daily Graphic, Wednesday November 21st, 1984, pp 1, 8.
85. Ibid
86. Daily Graphic, Friday April 26th, 1985, p.1.
87. Ibid
88. Kojo Vieta, Op.Cit. p. 125.
89. Interview with Ms. Joyce Aryee, Former PNDC Secretary for Information and then Education. Ms. Aryee who was also the special Assistant to the Chairman of the National Commission for Democracy was later given the position of Secretary for Local Government but she says she did not take that portfolio until she left the PNDC government in January, 1992.
90. Daily Graphic, November 7th, 1984 pp.1,8.
91. Daily Graphic, Friday October 14th, 1983 p.4.
92. Ibid
93. Interview with Ms. Joyce Aryee, Op Cit.

94. Daily Graphic Tuesday November 20th 1984, pp 1,5.
95. Daily Graphic, Tuesday December 10th, 1984, p.1.
96. Ibid
97. Ibid
98. Interview with Mrs. Kate Abbam, Publisher/Editor, Obaa Sima (Ideal Woman) Magazine, Thursday June 30th, 2005.
99. Daily Graphic, Tuesday April 9th, 1985, p.5.
100. Daily Graphic, Wednesday October 18th, 1989, p.1.
101. Daily Graphic, Tuesday April 9th, 1985, p.5.
102. Daily Graphic, Wednesday October 18th, 1989, p.1.
103. Theresa Larteley Lartey, "Women in Ghanaian Politics 1951 – 1990", An undergraduate dissertation presented to the Department of History, University of Ghana, Legon, Jne 1991, p.34.
104. Theresa Larteley Lartey, Op. Cit. p.35.
105. Daily Graphic, Saturday October 28th, 1989, p.8.
106. Ibid
107. Daily Graphic, Tuesday October 31st, 1989, p.1.
108. Ibid
109. Daily Graphic, Tuesday November 7th, 1989, p.8.
110. Ibid
111. Interview with Miss Joyce Aryee, Op.Cit
112. Daily Graphic, Saturday December 9th, 1989, p.3.
113. Daily Graphic, Tuesday December 19th, 1989, p.9.
114. Ibid
115. Interview with Kwaku Baako Jnr., Op Cit.
116. Daily Graphic, Saturday December 30th, 1989, p.3.
117. Daily Graphic, Thursday December 21st, 1989, p.3. Also, Daily Graphic, Tuesday November 14th, 1989 p.3.
118. Daily Graphic, Tuesday October 10th, 1989, p.3. Also, Daily Graphic, Friday November 17th, 1989 p.3.
119. 120.   Daily Graphic, Wednesday November 8th, 1989, p.3.
120. Ibid
121. Interview with Miss Joyce Aryee, Op. Cit.
122. Theresa Larteley Lartey, Op. Cit, p.35.

CONCLUSION

Women have played an important role in the politics of Ghana since independence. This has been in spite of the general perception of women as subordinate role players in the Ghanaian society. This perception has even not been as formidable as the paradox of a matrilineal system of inheritance and a patriarchal society attendant upon it. Another aspect of the Ghanaian society that has not helped women is the assignment of domestic chores. Domestic chores have largely been the customarily assigned responsibility of women thus contributing to cut them out effectively from the exercise of political functions which are usually exercised outside the setting of the domestic environment. These chores and their effect on women's chances in politics do not apply uniformly to all Ghanaian societies. It is the unique historical experiences of these societies that have informed their treatment of women. One aspect, however, remains uniform and this is the fact that as far as the traditional assignment of domestic chores is concerned, women are more burdened than men. The naturally assigned biological functions of babymaking and child–nurturing have also jointly been one of the barriers to women and their desire to participate in politics. Again, one can also talk about the expectations of traditional societies in terms of the general roles for women. Women are constantly faced with the traditionally expected functions of being a daughter, a mother, a wife, a sister and a contributor to household income all at one and the same time. In most cases, they have no options. Where they have, they are limited in choice. This is because the seeming availability of choice only presents women with the choice of being considered conformists or deviants.

The perception of women as the unequals of men transcends patrilineal societies and stretches often into matrilineal societies. This is a perception that has been a realistic part of the socio-political philosophy of the generality of Ghanaians thus even making it difficult for people, especially some males, to accept a woman as a leader. The various women who carved political roles for themselves within the 1957-

1992 period did so against the backdrop of the existence of this socio-political philosophy. Too many women exposed the frivolity of this perception and demonstrated that indeed when given the opportunity women could be as capable as men. In the pre-independence era, Nana Yaa Asantewaa of Edweso (Ejisu) in Asanteman and Okyehene Dokuaa in Akyem Abuakwa were some of the women that exemplified feminine military and political capabilities.

The pronunciation of the Atlantic Charter in 1945 was partly responsible for widespread anti-colonial activities aimed at the renunciation of colonialism the world over. In what was later to become Ghana, the United Gold Coast Convention and the Convention People's Party became the political mass movements that were used as the vehicles of anti-colonial activities. The latter gained pre-eminence and attracted Sophia Oboshie Doku, Hannah Cudjoe and Akua Asabea Ayisi among several other women. These women did contribute a great deal to the attainment of independence.

With independence attained, President Nkrumah successfully pushed for the passing of an affirmative action–type legislation to purposefully make ten women members of the new parliament of the Republic. This, though criticized, afforded the House the opportunity of benefiting from the ideas, suggestions and contributions of the fairer sex. The Nkrumah experiment was enhanced and the number of women was increased to eighteen in 1965 when Ghana became a one-party state resulting in the proscription of opposition parties.

The fall of Nkrumah the following year razed the foundation he had laid for women to the ground. Within the three years of its rule, the nearest women came to participating in the government of the National Liberation Council was the inclusion of Akua Asabea Ayisi, Ayishetu Ibrahim and Ruby Quartey-Papafio as members of the National Advisory Committee of the National Liberation Council. As has already been mentioned in this work, the National Liberation Council did little to liberate Ghanaian women.

The second Republic was also one of the worst regimes for women as far as access, representation and participation in government and politics was concerned. Catherine Katuni Tedam and Lydia Akanbodiipo-Kugblenu were the only Members of Parliament. The latter represented

Chiana–Paga whilst the former represented Sandema constituency. They, however, made a lot of useful contributions to the deliberations of the House.

Perhaps the worst military regime for women in terms of recognition and appointment to political positions was the National Redemption Council. This regime did not appoint any woman into top national position. Ironically, this was a regime that received a lot of support from Ghanaian women. Its offshoot, the supreme Military Council, however, appointed Gloria Nikoi to head the Foreign Affairs Ministry.

The Armed Forces Revolutionary Council cannot be roped into any fair analysis (which of course includes some comparisons and contrast making) of the political role of women in the various regimes because of its short life span and the caretaker nature of its outlook. It did not assign itself a political role per se. As has already been mentioned in this text, it concerned itself with its "house-cleaning".

The third republic saw the re-birth of parliamentary democracy in Ghana. The elections that were organized in 1979 saw five gallant women entering parliament. They did contribute to discussions on a variety of national issues thereby justifying their presence in the House.

The Provisional National Defence Council, the last military government in Ghana (and hopefully the last in the history of Ghana), saw the rebirth of vigorous women's participation in politics. Ama Ata Aidoo, Joyce Aryee, Aanaa Enin, Efua Sutherland Addy, Gertrude Zakaria, Mary Grant and Vida Yeboah were some of the women whose influence and contribution helped the sustenance of the Council. It is worthy of mention that there has never been any legislation in Ghana (especially in the post–colonial era) debarring women from taking part in politics. In all the instances of constitutional rule, for example, sexual equality in terms of the enjoyment of rights including the right to participate in politics has been guaranteed. In military regimes, too, there was no dichotomy between the rights enjoyed by men on the one hand and the rights enjoyed by women on the other. In dealing with realistic and practical situations, however, constitutional guarantees of equality before the law, equality in respect of political participation and in the enjoyment of rights do not count for much. This is especially true when these guarantees have little or no effect on traditional and customary law.

With the notable exception of the regimes of Kwame Nkrumah and Jerry John Rawlings virtually no governmental efforts were made in the 1957-1992 period to place women in the mainstream of national political activity. One can, to a considerable degree, therefore, say that both traditional systems and contemporary political systems of the post-colonial era have not acted to encourage women to take part in active politics albeit covertly.

The activities of non-governmental and other feminist-oriented organisations especially in the post–1975 period played a role in the re-awakening of both government and women themselves as far as political participation was concerned. This is one of the interpretations that can be given to the upsurge of the number of women in politics in the 1981–1992 period.

Another aspect of the question of women's involvement in politics in Ghana in the 1957-1992 period which accounts for differences in the treatment of women is the peculiar nature of the regime or government. It can be said that the treatment of women under the various regimes depended on the degree of elitism in the government. In the military governments of the National Liberation Council, National Redemption Council and Supreme Military Council which were very elitist, women were to a very large extent not made an integral part of government and this affected their political standing. This is because under those regimes the only way, one could play a part in politics was to be a part, directly or indirectly, of the government. This is in view of the fact that political opposition was not guaranteed under those regimes. In fact, political opposition was proscribed. Viewed from another perspective, one can say that it was only those in government who could take part in politics.

The second and third republican regimes also had semblances of elitism. The intellectual elite were predominant in the former whilst the old political elite dominated the latter. What perhaps provided some respite for women was the presence in those regimes of parliaments that afforded all citizens, including women, the opportunity to occupy seats and partake in deliberations. This saw some women taking up those opportunities. The difference between all the governments mentioned above on one hand and the governments of Nkrumah and Rawlings' PNDC on the other hand buttresses this argument of elitism accounting for the treatment of women.

These two former leaders of Ghana saw their governments as revolutions and decided to bring on board all manner of people. One needed not to be an intellectual to have a place in the government of Nkrumah. The same can be said about the government of Rawlings under the Provisional National Defence Council. The result was that in these two regimes, women occupied a pride of place and made a greater contribution to the political and governmental affairs of the country.

Too many women have indeed played great political roles in Ghana. This is especially true when one resists the temptation of analyzing the political role of women in a vacuum but rather looks at the situation within the context of all the barriers already mentioned.

From all that has been said in this work about firstly the concept of politics and secondly the various aspects of politics that this work has treated, it is agreeable that in future, a lot more research need to be done. For instance, research has to be conducted into the activities of the various women foot soldiers of the first, second and third republics who never made it to Parliament. Another area yawning to be filled is an academic investigation into the personality and political contribution of Nana Konadu Agyeman Rawlings; the single most influential First Lady in the post-colonial history of Ghana

Also, the activities of women appointed to leadership positions in local government as chief executives of districts need to be studied. There is also the need to research into the activities of women in ambassadorial positions and the activities of women in opposition parties. This is because even though all these areas fall under the collective broad definition of politics, they were clearly outside the scope of the operationalised definition of politics upon which this work has entirely been based.

BIBLIOGRAPHY

DISSERTATION
1. Lartey, Theresa L. "Women In Ghanaian Politics (1951-1990)", Dept. of History, University of Ghana, Legon, 1991.
2. Leslie, Nelson "The Role of Women in Post–Independent Ghana: Steps Towards Equality", Dept. of History, University of Ghana, Legon, 1996.

ORAL SOURCES
1. Interview with Kwaku Baako Jnr. On 18th June, 2005. Kwaku Baako is Editor, Crusading Guide newspaper and son of Kofi Baako, Minister of state in the First Republic.

2. Interview with Mrs. Kate Abbam on 23rd June, 2005. Mrs. Abbam is Publisher / Editor, Obaa Sima (Ideal Woman) Magazine; a magazine devoted to the writing and articulation of women's issues.

3. Interview with Miss Joyce Rosalind Aryee on 20th July, 2005. Miss Aryee was Provisional National Defence Council Secretary for Information and later Education. She was also the special Assistant to the Chairman of the National Commission for Democracy. She was later given the position of secretary for Local Government but she says she did not take that portfolio.

4. Interview with Mrs. Cecilia Kotey, Lecturer, Department of Ghanaian Languages, University of Cape Coast in December, 2004. Discussion centred on role of Ga women in traditional politics.

OFFICIAL REPORTS

1. Ghana Parliamentary Debates, Official report – First series, Vol. 20, 2nd July –5th September, 1960

2. Ghana Parliamentary Debates, Official Report – First Series, Vol. 22, 7th February- 10th March, 1961

3. Ghana Parliamentary Debates, Official Report – First Series, Vol. 24, 4th July – 3rd August, 1961.

4. Ghana Parliamentary Debates, Official Report – First Series, Vol. 26, 16th January – 16th February, 1962.

5. Ghana Parliamentary Debates, Official Report, - First Series, Vol. 31, 26th February – 5th April, 1963

6. Ghana Parliamentary Debates, Official Report – First Series, Vol. 32, 18th June – 5th July 1963.

7. Ghana Parliamentary Debates, Official Report – First Series, Vol. 40, 10th June – 17th September, 1965.

8. Ghana Parliamentary Debates, Official Report – Second Series, Vol.2, 17th February – 25th March 1970.

9. Ghana Parliamentary Debates, Official Report – Second Series, Vol. 3, 12th May – 26th June, 1970.

10. Ghana Parliamentary Debates, Official Report – Second Series, Vol. 4, 28th July – 18th September, 1970

11. Ghana Parliamentary Debates, Official Report – Second Series, Vol. 5, 10th November – 18th December, 1970.

12. Ghana Parliamentary Debates, Official Report – Second Series, Vol. 6, 23rd February – 5th May, 1971.

13. Ghana Parliamentary Debates, Official Report – Second Series, Vol. 7, 15th June – 13th July, 1971.

14. Ghana Parliamentary Debates, Official Report – Third Series, Vol. 5, 20th January – 27th March, 1981.

15. Ghana Parliamentary Debates, Official Report – Thrid Series, Vol. 6, 29th April – 21st August, 1981.

16. "From Beijing to Beijng + 5" Review and Appraisal of the Beijing Platform for Action (PFA): Report of the Secretary–General, United Nations, New York, 2001.

17. Ghana Gazette, January, July August, 1967

18. Ghana Gazette, June – December 1969

19. Ghana Gazette, January – December, 1978

20. Ghana Gazette, January – December, 1979

21. Ghana Gazette, January – June, 1980

22. Ghana Gazette, January – December 1982

UNOFFICIAL REPORTS

1. Africa Dairy: Weekly Record of Events in Africa, Vol. II, 1967

2. Keesing's Contemporary Archives (1971-1972), Vol. XVIII, Keesing's Publication Ltd, London, Keynsham BS 18 2BD, Bristol

3. Keesing's Contemporary Archives (1974), Vol. XX, Keesing's Publications Ltd, Longman Group Ltd, London.

BOOKS

1. Adamafio, Tawia, By Nkrumah's Side: The Labour And The Wounds, West Coast Publishing, 1982, Accra.

2. Adu, Boahen A; Ghana: Evolution and Change in the Nineteenth and Twentieth Centuries, Sankofa Educational Publishers, 2000, Accra

3. Adu Boahen A. (ed) UNESCO General History of Africa, Vol. VII. Heinemann Educational Books Ltd. 1985, London.

4. Affrifah, Kofi The Akyem Factor in Ghana's History, Ghana University Press, 2000, Accra.

5. Agbodeka, Francis (Ed) A Handbook of Eweland Vol. I, Woeli Publishing Services, 1997, Accra.

6. Amadiume, Ifi, Re-inventing Africa, Zed Books, 1997, London,

7. Arhin, Kwame (ed), The Life And Work of Kwame Nkrumah, Sedco Publishing, 1991, Accra.

8. Bluwey, Gilbert Keith, Political Science: An Introduction, Anansesem Publications, 1993, Accra

9. Brown, C.K, Women in Local Government: A case study of Central Region, Friedrich Ebert Foundation, 1996, Accra.

10. Busia Kofi Abrefa, The Position of the Chief In the Modern Political Systems of Ashanti; Oxford University Press, 1951, London.

11. Cammack, Paul et al; Third World Politics: A Comparative Introduction Macmillan, 1988, London.

12. Coulter, Edwin M. Principles of Politics and Government; 3rd Edition, Allyn and Bacon Inc. 1987, Boston.

13. Cutrufelli, Maria Rosa, Women of Africa: Roots of Oppression, Zed Press, 1983, London

14. Danquah, Moses, The Birth of The Second Republic, Editorial and Publishing Services, 1969, Accra

15. Danso–Boafo, Kwaku, A Political Biography of Kofi Abrefa Busia Ghana Universities Press, 1996, Accra.

16. Gyimah–Boadi E (Ed), Ghana Under PNDC Rule, CODESRIA, 1993

17. Hanson, Emmanuel & Ninsin, Kwame (Ed) The State, Development and Politics in Ghana, CODESRIA Book Series, 1989, London.

18. Hay, Margaret Jean & Stitcher, Sharon (ed) African Women South of the Sahara, Longman, 1984, London.

19. Kakabadse, Andrew & Parker Christopher (ed), Power, Politics and Organizations: A Behavioural Science View, John Wiley & Sons Ltd.,1984, London.

20. Little, Kenneth, African Women In Towns: An Aspect of Africa's Social Revolution, Oxford Universities Press, 1973, Cambridge

21. Magstadt, Thomas and Schotten, Peter, M. Understanding Politics: Ideas, Institutions and Issues, Martins Press, 1984, New York

22. Niane,D.T.(ed),UNESCO General History of Africa, Vol.IV, Heinemann Educational Books Ltd, London.

23. Ninsin, Kwame, Drah, F. K., Political Parties and Democracy in Ghana's Fourth Republic, Woeli Publishing Services, 1993, Accra.

24. Nnoli, Okwudiba, Introduction to Politics, Longman Group Ltd, 1986.

25. Oppong, Christine (ed), Female and Male in West Africa, Allen and Unwin, 1983, London.

26. Oyugi, Walter O. (ed) Democratic Theory and Practice, Heinemann Educational Books Inc., 1988, London.

27. Pellow, Deborah, Women In Accra: Options for Autonomy, Reference Publications Inc., 1977, U.S.A.

28. Rattray Ashanti; Oxford University Press, 1923, London.

29. Romero, Patricia W. Life Histories of African Women, The Ashfield Press, 1988, London.

30. Shillington, Kevin, Ghana and the Rawlings Factor, Macmillan Press Ltd. 1992, London.

31. Tsikata, Dzodzi (ed) General Training in Ghana: Politics, Issues and Tools, Woeli Publishing Services, 2001, Accra.

32. Uchendu, P. K., The Role of Nigerian Women in Politics: Past and

33. Present, Fourth Dimension Publishing Co. Ltd., 1993, Nigeria.

34. Vieta, Kojo, The Flagbearers of Ghana, ENA Publications, 2000, Accra.

35. Waddy, Chris, Women in Muslim History, Longman, 1980 London.

ARTICLES

1. Yusuf, Bilkisu, "Nigerian Women in Politics: Problems and Prospects" published in Women in Nigeria Today (a publication of papers at a seminar held at Ahmadu Bello University, Zaria, May 1982 and Published in 1985 by Zed Books Ltd.)

2. M'bow, Amadou-Mahtar, "Towards a new order with regard to the status of women" in Women - From Witch-hunt to politics (a selection of articles reproduced from "cultures-dialogue between the peoples of the world" published in 1985 by UNESCO).

3. "Market women hail the coup" Daily Graphic, January 21, 1972

4. "Ghana International Ladies Friendship Association", Obaa Sima (Ideal Woman)Magazine, July, 1972, Vol. 1 No. 12.

5. "Lives of Achievement", Obaa Sima (Ideal Woman) Magazine, July/August, 1973.

6. "Seminar on Women" Obaa Sima (Ideal Woman) Magazine, August 1975.

7. "Africa and the Women's Liberation Movement", Obaa Sima (Ideal Woman) Magazine, October 1975.

8. "What is Zonta International", Obaa Sima (Ideal Woman) Magazine, January/February 1996.

9. "Makola Women's Association call on General Acheampong", Daily Graphic, July 23rd, 1977.

10. "Beware of These Women" Daily Graphic, July 28, 1977.

11. "General Acheampong meets executive body of the NCWD", Daily Graphic, August 10, 1977.

12. "Market women warned", Daily Graphic, August 13, 1977.

13. "A-G Relieved of post", Daily Graphic, January 2, 1979.

14. "Canadian Envoy is feted", Daily Graphic, January 5, 1979

15. "More grease madam", Daily Graphic, January 8, 1979

16. "Heads of ministries appointed", Daily Graphic, January 22, 1982.

17. "Three New Secretaries", Daily Graphic, January 1, 1982.

18. "Secretaries, Deputies named", Daily Graphic, February 2, 1982.

19. "Creative Activities In Children will be developed" Daily Graphic, February 25, 1982.

20. "Women Urged to compete with Men", Daily Graphic, March 18, 1982.

21. "Train School Children to be Patristic Ms. Aidoo", Daily Graphic, March 19, 1982.

22. "Women and the Revolution", Daily Graphic, April 28, 1982.

23. "Ghanaian Women", Daily Graphic, May 4, 1982.

24. "December 31 Movement Launched", Daily Graphic, May 17, 1982.

25. "Send Wards to Public Schools", Daily Graphic, May 19, 1982.

26. "Education should not be a Barrier", Daily Graphic, July 10, 1982.

27. "Changes made in the Cabinet", Daily Graphic, July 29, 1982.

28. "Two PNDC Members Resign" Daily Graphic, August 19, 1982.

29. "Play down petty jealousies-Zakaria" Daily Graphic, August 25, 1982.

30. "Help improve school system - Ms. Aidoo", Daily Graphic, August 30, 1982.

31. "Women have a part to play in the Revolution", Daily Graphic, August 30, 1982.

32. "Women's Groups Urged to Unite", Daily Graphic, September 7, 1982

33. "Paper can be Milled on Small-Scale", Daily Graphic, October 1, 1982.

34. "Social Transformation is our Aim", ", Daily Graphic, October, 1982.

35. "Educate Masses on Local Food" ", Daily Graphic, October 16, 1982.

36. "Ghana, Ivory Coast Must Help Freedom Fighters" Daily Graphic, October 29, 1982.

37. "Invest in Education", Daily Graphic, April 2, 1985.

38. "Protect Ghana's Canopy of Forest–Timber Operators Told," Daily Graphic, April 8, 1985.

39. "Regional Secretary" Daily Graphic, April 9, 1985.

40. "Decision on District Councils Won't Change", Daily Graphic, April 17, 1985.

41. "Marked Improvement Anticipated", Daily Graphic, April 25, 1985.

42. "Czech Aid to Ghana Commended", Daily Graphic, April 26, 1985.

43. "Japan's example worth emulating – Joyce", Daily Graphic, October 4, 1983.

44. "Aussie Envoy calls on Joyce", Daily Graphic, October 14, 1983.

45. "Aanaa Advises Christians", Daily Graphic, October 15, 1984.

46. "Form co-ops, Ghanaian women told", Daily Graphic, October 16, 1984.

47. "Soap Factory Commissioned", Daily Graphic, October 22, 1984.

48. "Mrs. Rawlings Advises Youth", Daily Graphic, October 29, 1984

49. "Let's set the pace –Joyce", Daily Graphic, October 31, 1984

50. "Joyce-Government Is Doing Its Best", Daily Graphic, November 7, 1984

51. "Mrs. Alhassan Confers With Two Envoys", Daily Graphic, November 7, 1984

52. "Changes In Portfolio", Daily Graphic, November 12, 1984

53. "The Youth On Peace March", Daily Graphic, November 20, 1984

54. "Ghana's Food Storage Problem", Daily Graphic, November 21, 1984

55. "Use The Media To Arm The People", Daily Graphic, December 3, 1984

56. "Children's Park For BA Region", Daily Graphic, December 17m, 1984

57. "Women's Participation In National Economy", Daily Graphic, December 17, 1984

58. "The World Needs Peace To Develop....Says Joyce Aryee", Daily Graphic, December 18, 1984

59. "PNDC Is Committed To True Democracy-Joyce Aryee", Daily Graphic, January 4, 1988

60. "FAO To Assist Women Increase Food Production", Daily Graphic, January 14, 1988

61. "Working Women Urged To Show Sense of Competence", Daily Graphic, February 1, 1988

62. "Mrs. De Cuellar Calls On Nana Agyeman Rawlings", Daily Graphic, February 10, 1988

63. "African Women Urged To Win More Successes", Daily Graphic, February 10, 1988

64. "Women's Movement Making Grains In Tumu Area", Daily Graphic, February16, 1988

65. "In defence of A Page About Women", Daily Graphic, February 18, 1988.

66. "Insurance seminar for market women", Daily Graphic, February 20, 1988

67. "Women For Change", Daily Graphic, February 25, 1988

68. "First Ladies Exchange Solidarity Greetings", Daily Graphic, March 7, 1988

69. "Produce High Quality Goods For Public", Daily Graphic, March 8, 1988

70. "Government Has Political Direction", Daily Graphic, April 4, 1988

71. "A Fitting Incentive", Daily Graphic, April 4, 1988

72. "Major Changes In Government", Daily Graphic, April 5, 1988

73. "Let's Free Nation From Economic Stagnation" Daily Graphic, April 7, 1988

74. "Unite And Work For National Progress", Daily Graphic, May 9, 1988.

75. "Dismantle The Inhuman System Of Apartheid", Daily Graphic, May 18, 1988

76. "Adopt A More Dynamic Attitude, Women Advised", Daily Graphic, May 20, 1988

77. "Join 31st DWM", Daily Graphic, May 23, 1988

78. "Change Negative Attitude, for Success of Revolution", Daily Graphic, May 18, 1988

79. "Sampa 31st DWM Mount Campaign", Daily Graphic, May 27, 1988

80. "Obeng, Aanaa honoured", Daily Graphic, June 11, 1988

81. "Women's Movement Educate Women", Daily Graphic, June 20, 1988

82. "Undertake Viable Economic Ventures", Daily Graphic, June 25, 1988

83. "Lead exemplary Lives, teachers told", Daily Graphic, June 27, 1988

84. "Pool Resources For Development", Daily Graphic, October 10, 1989

85. "Encourage More Women To Acquire Knowledge", Daily Graphic, October 11, 1989

86. "Explore Avenues To Strengthen National Service Scheme", Daily Graphic, October 16, 1989

87. "One JSS In Each District To Be Upgraded", Daily Graphic, October 18, 1989

88. "Ensure Fullest Participation of Women In Economic Activities", Daily Graphic, October 21, 1989.

89. "Aanaa Relieved of Duties as PNDC Member", Daily Graphic, October 25, 1989

90. "Prevent Youth From Indulging In Drug Abuse", Daily Graphic, October 28, 1989

91. "Government Determined To Fight Menace of Drug Abuse", Daily Graphic, October 31, 1989

92. "Educate Couples On Population And Family Life Issues- Grant", Daily

93. Graphic, November 7, 1989

94. "Oteng Launches Cultural Programme", Daily Graphic, November 8, 1989

95. "Asante-Akim North Assembly Spends ₡8.8m on Dev. Programme", Daily Graphic, November 10, 1989

96. "Public Education Committee Reconstituted", Daily Graphic, November 14, 1989

97. "Show sense of commitment to development – Bus-Kwofie", Daily Graphic, November 17, 1989

98. "Submit Your Budgetary Proposals On Time", Daily Graphic, December 9, 1989

99. "Support Efforts At Helping Destitutes In Society", Daily Graphic, December 19, 1989

CPSIA information can be obtained at www.ICGtesting.com
Printed in the USA
LVOW11s0424141014

408538LV00001B/230/P